Wings of Rapture

Nema

BLACK MOON PUBLISHING
CINCINNATI, OHIO USA

Black Moon Manifesto

It is the Will and mission of Bate Cabal/Black Moon to effectively manifest unique and insightful occult Works for the esoteric community in a manner that is unfettered by commercial considerations.

Copyright © 2020 Michael Ingalls

Cover design copyright © 2020 Black Moon Publishing, LLC

All rights reserved.

BlackMoonPublishing.com

blackmoonpublishing@gmail.com

Design and layout by
Jo Bounds of Black Moon

ISBN: 978-1-890399-75-7

United States • United Kingdom • Europe • Australia • India • Japan

CONTENTS

Foreword 5
Introduction 13
1   What Is Known Is Not Enough 17
2   God-Hunger and Other Forgotten Ones 23
3   Cosmophilia 39
4   Maat Magick 49
5   Emotions 59
6   Temple-Time and Nature 67
7   Inventory and Corrections 83
8   Mantram and Silence 91
9   Call and Forget 95
10 Manifestations: Signs of Progress 101
11 Unlearned Knowledge 107
12 Astral Adventures 119
13 Cosmic Visions 129
14 Veils of Glory 141
15 Self 153
16 Shadow Mirror 167
17 That 181
18 The Inner Life 187

19 Dark Night of the Soul	193
20 Alone Together	201
21 The View From Now	213
N'Aton: Visions of the Major Arcana	225
Appendix A: Liber Pennae Praenumbra	257
Appendix B: Feathersong	269
Glossary	283
Bibliography	297
Index	301

Foreword

Foreword

I was both surprised and honored when asked to write the foreword for this book. I have had the great pleasure of knowing Nema for more than a decade. Well, actually, that is not quite accurate. I have known her for that long, but I have known of her for a quarter of a century—it was about twenty-five years ago that I read her writings (under the name Andahadna) in the first issues of *The Cincinnati Journal of Ceremonial Magick*.

What an amazing, exciting time that was! For a long time, Magick had disappeared into tiny dens and was left to people who prided themselves on dogmatically repeating what had been done before. Even though the final volume of Regardie's classic four-volume set, *The Golden Dawn*, had completed publication in 1940, it had languished on shelves. It took almost thirty years for the second, two-volume edition to appear. The same was true of many of the works of Aleister Crowley. The first books on modern Wicca and witchcraft were beginning to appear.

In the late sixties and early seventies, a spiritual renaissance had begun. Confounding the dogmatists who looked back to the "simpler" time of the 1950s (ignoring the racism, anti-Semitism, extreme poverty, and diseases such as polio, which wracked the U.S. at the time to a far greater level than most people today could believe), this new spiritual occult movement had no leader. Instead, it had many leaders.

Some of those leaders, and some independent people, simply replayed what went before. But others asked impossible questions such as "Why?" and "What if?" Answers such as "It's

tradition," or "It's always been done that way," could no longer be accepted. This meant personal research and investigation. This meant that reading wasn't enough. Instead, Magick was returning to its core of being an experimental science.

For those of you reading this who know Nema, no introduction is necessary. For those of you who are unfamiliar with her writing, I could never say enough. Nema was—and is—one of those incredibly unique magickal thinkers. She not only asked (and continues to ask) "Why?" but helped forge new directions in the actual practice of magick. If you are ever talking about topics such as ceremonial Magick, Aleister Crowley, Kenneth Grant, and being a practitioner of Magick, you should—you must—include her valuable contributions to the field.

So why is it, then, that you may not have heard of her? Much like the work of Bardon, people use her concepts, techniques, and information without crediting her. In her previous major work, *Maat Magick*, she literally tore the lid off the concepts of Magickal limitations, arguing for being able to use any form of Magick from any of the aeons of time. She gave information on how to make Magick truly usable with an eclecticism that was not only practical, but defied virtually all previous (mis)conceptions of the Magickal art.

The work you hold in your hands is also groundbreaking, but in a totally different direction. Or rather, it should be a parallel path to those who practice—as opposed to those who only theorize or talk about—Magick, the ability to cause desired changes in your personal universe. To fully describe it requires a bit of background.

I have been involved in Magick for... well, for a long time. I live and breathe incense. I have long said that "Magick is not something you do, Magick is something you are." I have been striving

Foreword

to achieve that goal. During this process, I found that some of the techniques I had learned–techniques that had previously been valuable–were no longer important to me. I wondered, *Is that all there is?* This eventually led me in new Magickal directions culminating in my book, *Modern Sex Magick* (to which Nema graciously contributed a valuable article).

In that book, I partially answered that question. In this book you will find the full answer to that question. And whether you are involved in the practice of Magick or not, eventually you will come to ask yourself that other question: "Why am I here?"

This question does not have a single, simple answer. It opens the door to numerous other questions. What was I before I was born? What will happen to me after I die? What is the secret nature of the universe? How do I find meaning in my life? Is there a God or gods, and if so, how do I contact Him/Her/It/Them? Is contact even possible?

I was once talking to a friend who is a Jungian therapist. I pointed out that Freud had described certain needs of each human: survival, reproduction, and so on. I wondered if there was also a need to be spiritual in some way. She responded that Jung thought the desire for spirituality was also a primal need.

In one of the most interesting sections of this book, Nema describes these basic, primal urges as the "Forgotten Ones." She includes sex, fight-or-flight, clanning, hunger, communication, altruism, curiosity, and "God-hunger." She calls them "Forgotten Ones" (certainly recalling a Lovecraftian theme) because, for the most part, we ignore these urges in our lives. Perhaps the most important of the survival instincts for this foreword is the God-hunger.

As humans, we need some way to be in contact with some-

thing that is greater than us. In many rather stuffy books that are available on the subject, this drive is known as Mysticism, the study and practice of having a direct relationship with the Divine. This study, as usually presented, is often tedious, dated, and limiting. For many of us, the Divine–God–is that "old bearded dude on a throne in the clouds." For those who have broader view, God may be a force, or energy. But still, this is limiting because God is "out there" and separate from us. In philosophy and theology this is known as a transcendent deity. Even with a deity who is standing in front of us, there is still that occasional painful separation.

There should be more. Can we not find the beauty and magnificence of the Divine in the physical universe around us? Is it not also found in mathematics and theoretical physics? There is something there that defies any sort of limitation or categorization–but it is there! It is the Mystery that hides achingly behind the façade of material solidity in our physical world. It is the mystery that drove people to ask, "What are subatomic particles made of and how do they function?" and which in turn led to string theory and the concept that the universe is constantly flashing between being waves and particles with data, the theory of the holographic universe. But what is beyond that? What is beyond the mathematical equations and theories of the genius Ramanujian, and why did he suffer so?

And when we finally discover solutions to those questions, what lies beyond that? We are left with mystery upon mystery. Eventually, by peeling away the small mysteries, like petals of a rose, we may eventually come to experience, in a blinding flash or an orgasmic sigh, the ultimate Mystery. And it is this Mystery that is the subject and driving force behind this book.

This brings me back to Magick. The fact is, many (if not

most) people who come to practice Magick do so for one reason: power over others. They want it quickly and they want it to be strong. Unfortunately for most of them (and fortunately for the rest of us!), they quickly discover that merely reading words out of a book doesn't cut the mustard. Magick—real Magick—takes practice and dedication. It's not like you see in the movies. Disappointed, some of these people turn to other practices, such as Neuro-Linguistic Programming, only to discover, again, that NLP also takes practice, intuition, and dedication.

Those who stick with Magick generally make an incredible discovery. Magick can bring you a great deal of power: but it is power over yourself, not others. Indeed, *Wings of Rapture* (previously titled *The Way of Mystery*) is also very much a book about the heart and soul of Magick, and many important techniques and concepts are revealed in a way that only Nema can express, both "down home" and with the stars. As part of your magickal practices, you will discover that there is a greater reality to the universe, as well as to the very essence of who and what you are, than you could have possibly imagined before. What is this greater reality? Lots of people have described it in a variety of ways. People are still arguing about it today. The ultimate nature of this greater reality remains a mystery to those who have not experienced it. But how can you do that?

This book has some of the answers, but not all of them, thankfully. If it had all of them it would remove the very essence of the fact that the answer is a mystery. Not a mystery in the sense of Agatha Christie or Inspector Columbo, but Mystery in the sense of our awe-filled amazement and feelings over the wonder that is the universe. Keys to self-examination given here unlock the inner mysteries, too.

Mystery, as presented here, is an expansion on previous

concepts of mysticism. Thus, the information here will help you get closer to the Divine. It will also help you learn more about yourself, why you are here, and your part in the plan of the cosmos.

This is not really a book about Nema, although she bravely shares intimate details of her life in order to help you on your path. Nor is it really a book that is just about the Mystery. Rather, it is a book about you. Nema has broken the ground and now shows you how to follow this journey as a parallel path to *your* Magickal path. She shares some of the marvels you are likely to encounter and reveals pitfalls so you can be prepared and not lose focus.

Imagine, for a second, taking an empty bookshelf and placing a separator in the middle. If you label the left side "My Most Important Magickal Texts," chances are good that you would be able to easily fill that side and have books left over. If you labeled the right side "My Most Important Books for Magickal Spiritual Growth," this book might be alone on that side.

To really discuss all of the practical, philosophical, theological, and mind-expanding techniques, concepts, and ideas revealed here would require another book in itself. I honestly think that people—perhaps you—will be discussing the possibilities and practices in this book for years to come. Please don't read this book speedily and with no attention to detail, as if it were a novel. Instead, I encourage you to passionately savor Nema's elegant and lucid writing and use the ideas and concepts presented here to change your life. You will find that Nema never pushes you through a door, but she indicates, points, and sometimes nudges you in a lightly traveled (but now mapped) direction so you can eventually experience the majesty of the mystery yourself. Like the Hermit of the tarot, she shines a

Foreword

light. Bask in that light and select the unique path that will best allow you to explore the mystery.

– Donald Michael Kraig

Nema's work stands (and sometimes hangs during the inevitable Dark Night of the Soul) with Saint John of the Cross in terms of great mystical writings. Reading Nema, one is inspired to re/discover the mystical experience in the moment to moment to moment flow of existence...starry points of being tumbling into the great bardo only to find resurrection in the bright lucidity of mind. This book allows the reader to make this discovery therefore it sits as a holy text, a holy book; words with a cadence and meanings able to open the eyes of the soul.

This is a work that strikes a balance between the relevance and power of day and nightside to the developing and experienced mystic. Imbalance is the curse of the Mage or Mystic leading to attachment or aversion. Insights abound. Nema's description of the abyss can only be fully appreciated by those who have at least tasted the nausea that flows within life's unsure horizon. Ursula K. Le Guin once commented that her writing was the most universal when it relied on the most personal, the most individual of her experiences. Nema, in writing with an unerring honesty about the most personal of her experiences also reaches this universality.

The forward by Donald Michael Kraig was written for the original publication, *The Way of Mystery*, in 2003. This edition has been revised and expanded with the help of the author. The present title, *Wings of Rapture*, is much preferred by the author. – Ed.

Introduction

The way of Mystery is the process of exploring the transphysical realms for yourself. It's been a rare path in our past, reserved for saints and poets, shamans and visionaries. Many of our fellow humans are content with the prefabricated and packaged tenets of faith in an established religion, with the speculations of philosophers, or with the now-standard "alternative" practices of neopaganism, Wicca, Asatru, Eastern religions, various kinds of Magick, and so on. A Mystic is a maverick, sometimes by choice and sometimes by surprise, who appreciates other people's visions but is not satisfied by them.

The very fact that you've opened this book and are reading these words tells me that you are a seeker and explorer, curious, and not satisfied by pat answers. You probably have had brushes with the unseen. You prefer questions to answers and want direct experience rather than intellectual speculation.

Why should you read this book? That depends on where you are in your search of truth and wisdom, on the stage of transformation you find yourself in now. If you're relatively young in spirit, it could help you to save time by learning methods of exploration that are independent of faith, authority, and mystique. If you're in the thick of experimentation with established religions, Magickal Orders, covens, and/or bestselling gurus, it can help you slice through the embellishments of other people's visions to find your own. If you're a veteran of "the Path," it offers companionship by the campfire in an often desolate land.

What are the benefits, the practicalities for pursuing

Introduction

Mystery in exploring the unknown? What is the payoff?

The desire for and need of transcendence are as real and as necessary to our survival, as individuals and as a species, as are the more obvious instincts of hunger, self-preservation, and sex. Most of us are asleep to that fact, living in discontent and unease in the midst of plenty. This book presents techniques for recognizing and satisfying this desire and need.

As animals, mammals, and primates, we live at the mercy of conflicts between our more primitive instincts and those born of an increasingly complex intelligence and technology. The urge to procreate and multiply has run amok; our numbers destroy rainforests, pollute the planet we live on, and could make us extinct. Our intelligence can direct and manage our more basic drives when we understand the context of our existence. This book provides methods for achieving such understanding.

We're social animals as well as individuals, depending on each other for life and livelihood, companionship and help. Our sense of community was limited to our immediate surround before the advent of social web sites on the Internet. In the physical world, however, we still deal with limitations of distance. These limitations promote wars and genocide, allow governments and corporations to invest in sports arenas and amusements parks while children starve, and divide us into "races," genders, and believers who vie for social superiority and possession of resources. This book outlines a larger reality of self and community, a view broader and deeper than that which prevails among us now. You, an individual, can be a significant force for good and for change; your realizations influence the rest of us through our genetic link as well as through our shared racial unconscious.

We are not alone in the cosmos. There are other intelligences

Introduction

at our level of complexity, or at more complex levels, that wait for our conversation and our expansion beyond our home planet, and beyond species boundaries. In order to be able to understand the concepts that interest others, we need to experience the realities upon which the concepts are founded. This book offers the means to do so.

What can you expect in the following pages? An honest account of my own explorations, visions, trances and ecstasies; working hypotheses about life, the universe, and Nothing, and practices that make transphysical experiences easier. You can expect the early chapters to provide necessary background information. I was unable to rank these in importance or sequence because they're equally important and engage you in a variety of sequences. Stay with them and they'll click together in a way most meaningful to you.

When I describe a practice or technique, consider it as a recommendation that you should do likewise. In appropriate chapters, I give specific instructions on the practices I've mentioned. Experiment with the details of the methods, and adapt them to fit your individuality. There's a saying that "When the student is ready, the teacher will come." A book can be such a teacher.

This book is not a cookbook of recipes where doing A will always produce B. It is not "Mystery for Dummies," a grimoire, or a complete atlas of maps of the transphysical territories. It's as simple an account as I could make, written to encourage you to find your way to the truth of things. For me, it's an act of enlightened self-interest; for you, I hope it's a new understanding of "enlightened," of "self," and of "interest."

Don't take my word for it–come see for yourself.

Deep Mind

Chapter 1

What Is Known Is Not Enough

e come to the gates of Mystery, half driven and half drawn, suspended on a crest of longing, hope, fear, expectation and doubt. Suddenly or gradually, we find old resources of spiritual satisfaction and comfort are no longer able to guide us in our search for meaning in life, for the divine. Former certainties melt away; accumulating life experiences force us to question that which we had accepted. We're free-falling into chaos, grappling for a hold on reality.

It's as though faith slips away, leaving nothing in its place. It could be that faith had never been present, and we're now becoming aware of the void that faith could fill. If we rely on science to replace faith, disappointment is certain; science gives us observed physical events linked by hypotheses and theorems--all of which hint at the divine intelligence behind them--but offer little consideration of the nature of that intelligence. One tentative step that science has made in the direction of Mystery is the idea of the anthropic principle, which proposes that the laws governing subatomic physics are in their present form because humans exist to observe them. If the rules were different, we wouldn't exist.

Stephen Hawking, author of *A Brief History of Time*, says of this concept:

"The anthropic principle does provide some sort of

Chapter 1 :: What is Known is Not Enough

explanation of many of the remarkable numerical relations that are observed between the values of different physical parameters. However, it is not completely satisfactory; one cannot help feeling that there is some deeper explanation. Also, it cannot account for all the regions of the universe. For example, our solar system is certainly a prerequisite for our existence, as is an earlier generation of nearby stars in which heavy elements could have been formed by nuclear synthesis. It might even be that the whole of our galaxy was required. But there does not seem any necessity for other galaxies to exist, let alone the million million or so of them that we see distributed roughly uniformly throughout the observable universe. This large-scale homogeneity of the universe makes it very difficult to believe that the structure of the universe is determined by anything so peripheral as some complicated molecular structures on a minor planet orbiting a very average star in the outer suburbs of a fairly typical spiral galaxy." [1]

It's interesting and encouraging to see scientists dipping into the idea of first cause, even though the anthropic principle repeats the error of religionists in making man the measure of all things. We have our legitimate place on the planet and in the universe, but, in our present general level of comprehension, we're not the central figure nor the organizing principle. Science keeps itself honest through observation, experiment and prediction, and our body of physical knowledge grows daily through the work of dedicated scientists. An increasingly accurate knowledge of nature helps us comprehend the experiences that the pursuit of Mystery grants us; the more pieces we have of the puzzle, the better we can see its picture.

Philosophy offers intellectual speculation and individual surmise on human phenomena and natural law, relying on

Chapter 1 :: What is Known is Not Enough

reason to reach logical conclusions. Speculation and reason also have their place in the universe, although such functions can only produce belief, not knowledge. Some philosophies, like Marxism and Nazism, have failed miserably when employed as social policy; the fatal flaws in each were a misunderstanding of human nature and the implementing of policy with force. The philosophies enshrined in the Constitution of the United States of America, those of individual rights and limited governmental powers, seem to be working, in somewhat rough ways.

In the more abstract realms of philosophy, logical positivism, which denies the validity of metaphysical knowledge and accepts only provable facts as the basis of truth, seems to have reached an impasse with the discovery that the observer affects the experiment, that quantum theory introduces uncertainty into the nature of the universe. Existentialism, on the other hand, states that there are no absolute, objective truths, that ethics are self-derived, and moral responsibility for action and non-action rests with the individual. In my opinion, this coincides more closely with experiences of Mystery, save that the angst of the way of Mystery is of a different quality than that of existentialism.

Science and philosophy can be considered objective human pursuits. Scientists and philosophers work with subjects that aren't specifically human, such as mathematics, astronomy, and physics. Human behavioral sciences, such as psychology, sociology, history, anthropology, etc., are considered "soft" science since not all data involving them can be measured, quantified, qualified, or formulated. Philosophy is softer still, since it offers conclusions processed and produced by human thinking, which combines the findings of science, personal observations, and the works of great philosophers of the past

Chapter 1 :: What is Known is Not Enough

with all the quirks of the individual philosopher.

Art, in its many forms, is also a way of knowing. Some arts offer a type of objectivity, forms such as photography, cinematography, realism in painting, drawing and sculpture, and architecture. Other arts are, by nature, abstract and intuitive, like music, nonrepresentational painting and sculpture, and dance. The arts of word use a triple layer of symbolism--words represent things, acts, and states of being; printed characters grouped in certain ways represent words, and the things words represent are often metaphors for ideas other than their own common meanings.

Human individuality makes precision in transmitting ideas and their accompanying emotions impossible; we communicate in approximations. Even shared experiences are perceived through our separate identities' sensoria. Perhaps it is only in the realm of numbers that we really can convey ideas, and only through the Forgotten Ones, our hardwired survival instincts, can we convey emotions.

Individual sensory data, alone or aided by instruments, are the only means our consciousness has to learn about the cosmos around us, both immediately and through the information transmitted from other individuals. Surface-level introspection is usually verbalized by consciousness for purposes of processing and remembering; to go deeper into inner realities requires the abandonment of words altogether. Some call it the unconscious, or the subconscious, but I prefer the term "Deep Mind", courtesy of Jan Fries,[2] for that part of us which generates dreams and which operates on the pre-verbal and post-verbal levels.

Why are there barriers between waking consciousness and the Deep Mind? Why is it necessary for us to walk

Chapter 1 :: What is Known is Not Enough

any "path of initiation" in order for our parts to have free information exchange with each other? The other animals on this planet don't seem to have our problems; perhaps the very characteristics which distinguish *genus Homo* from the rest of the animal kingdom constitute the inner divisions which alienate us from ourselves.

What we know with our waking consciousness is not enough to satisfy the soul-hunger which spurs us to pursue God or Goddess, to search for the meaning of life, to desire personal continuity beyond the gates of death. To find the peace of satisfaction we must expand our means of knowledge beyond the limits of conscious mind and the spacetime continuum. From earliest shamanic practices to the latest methods of exploring the realms of spirit, we strive to surpass ourselves and our traditions in the search of ultimate truth.

Notes:
1. Stephen Hawking, *Black Holes and Baby Universes and Other Essays* (New York, NY: Bantam Books) 1993, page 52.
2. From private correspondence.

Chapter 2

God-Hunger and Other Forgotten Ones

hy do humans get religion? Why do we do Magick, cast runes, read Tarot cards, toss yarrow stalks for the I Ching, and throw cowrie shells? Why do we fast in the wilderness in pursuit of a vision, eat sacred mushrooms and peyote buttons, meditate in silence, sacrifice to feed our Loa, or to please our gods, channel entities from other worlds and times, and/or hope for an encounter with extraterrestrials?

The root of all these activities is a sense of needing help in learning to negotiate the spirit world, of hope for postmortem survival of our individuality and identity, and of a mixture of fear and curiosity about the unknown. We are aware of the spirit world through self-reflection, through dreams and through personal experience of events that seem to circumvent physical laws as we know them.

About twenty years ago, I was feeling sad and depressed about the loss of my father, who had died several years before. I was alone in the house, and was standing in the kitchen doorway, near the table. I suddenly felt a strong, warm presence, and a coin (a USA 25-cent piece) sailed past my face from behind my shoulder and bounced on the table. I turned around, but no one

Chapter 2 :: God-Hunger and Other Forgotten Ones

was there. The mint date on the quarter was 1965, the year of my father's death.

Other common phenomena include knowing who's calling when the phone rings, suddenly thinking about someone whom you haven't seen for a long time, then encountering him or her shortly afterward, having street lamps go dark as you pass underneath, and having accurate hunches on a steady basis.

PSI phenomena are the crazy aunties of science, kept in the attic and not discussed in polite conversation. Charles Fort,[1] author and researcher of unexplained phenomena, held that scientists refused to take seriously or to investigate reports of frogs, rocks, and other strange objects fallen from the sky, of accurate precognitive dreams, of coffins rearranged in a mausoleum, and other "damned things", because such events didn't fit their view of the possible. Instead of expanding the boundaries of the possible, the scientific authorities of his time rejected the truth of the events, their reporters, or both.

Fort collected and published a large number of odd, seemingly miraculous events, without formulating theories about them. While there have been attempts at investigating such PSI phenomena as telepathy, precognition and telekinesis, by organizations like the Rhine Institute of Duke University, and while I've encountered reports of psychics being tested by American intelligence agencies as potential spies,[2] there have been no sustained and serious civilian researches that I know of.

Professional psychics, water dowsers, rainmakers and fortune tellers cash in on their ability to use the nonmaterial realms of existence, but any normal human being has similar talents to a greater or lesser degree of development and training. Sometimes the Deep Mind shapes your dreams to

Chapter 2 :: God-Hunger and Other Forgotten Ones

deliver information you need, sometimes events occur in your waking hours that cause you to doubt the reality of the world of everyday life.

Whatever the sources of our information about it, humans generally accept the reality of the nonmaterial levels of life. We deal daily with symbols and concepts, nonmaterial things like honor, duty, loyalty and other virtues, with entities like families, corporations and governments, and with abstractions like mathematics, ethics, and opinions. Abstractions, concepts and symbols are living entities in their own planes, or levels of density, and in our dealings with them, we acquire a sense that their existence is as "real" as our own in their realm.

Humans are complex beings who live in many levels of density at the same time; sometimes we're aware of our multiple lives, but usually we have our consciousness immersed in the material universe. Our genetic programming directs our individual survival and the survival and evolution of our genus and species, so much of our thinking is about making a living, getting the shelter, clothes, transportation and the toys we feel we need, finding the perfect mate, raising a family, and healing our ailments.

For convenience's sake, I divide our survival program into eight urges, or Forgotten Ones: hunger, sex, flight or fight, clanning, communication, curiosity, altruism and God-hunger. The last one named, God-hunger, can be defined as the human impulse toward transcendence. These Forgotten Ones–forgotten, not in the lack of our awareness of them, but forgotten in that we rarely credit them with the influence they exert on our actions–build complexity from simplicity.

In conversations with the astral pattern of the human DNA molecule (part of walking in Mystery is learning about things

Chapter 2 :: God-Hunger and Other Forgotten Ones

from the things themselves), I gather that DNA is concerned with our genus as a whole, and that individuals are but means to its ends. The only times our molecular god is interested in individuals are when the occasional favorable mutation manifests or when individuals threaten the continuity and development of the genus and species. I understand that the same holds true for other living beings, and that the personalities of the variations of genetic structure represented by the many genera and species on earth have been called "devas".

Of course, there can be no species manifesting without the individuals who comprise it, just as we'd have no liver without liver cells nor a brain without its neurons. Our Forgotten Ones interact in a logical fashion to make elaborations of themselves.

Hunger is basic to the individual as sex is basic to the species. We eat to provide energy for motion, milk for our young, and substance to replace our aging and dying cells.

We mate and make babies to provide variation in DNA's manifestation and to replace the aging and dying individuals of our species. The concept of romantic love often serves as a mask for the raw power of sexual attraction.

The Forgotten One of fight-or-flight is an extension of the self-preservational nature of hunger and sex. Individuals need to stay alive in order to make babies and to defend them until they can survive on their own. Adults of our species, as well as adults of others, often risk and lose their lives in defense of infants and children.

With our dangerous lack of fangs, claws, horns or speed, we find it necessary to band together with others of our kind to make a living and to stay alive. "Blood is thicker than water," so our attachments are the strongest with those with whom we live, work, share danger, celebrate, and mourn. The Forgotten

Chapter 2 :: God-Hunger and Other Forgotten Ones

One of clanning is an active, rather than a reactive, instinct, and it assists us in feeding and defending individuals whom we accept as ours and as "us". The clan, as well as the family, tribe, and nation, provides dramatic tension and opportunities for strong emotions in the play of the more basic urges within its structure. Trade, wars, and intermarriage among different human groupings are generally beneficial to our genus, although the balance between enough and too much in any of these is delicate and easily knocked askew, usually by disparities in numbers or in technology.

The urge to communicate is born of all that has gone before it, and serves as a social glue as well as a means to accumulate, preserve and transmit knowledge from one generation to the next. The ability to use words, both spoken and written, is the first impulse of realizing and manifesting our conscious unity as a genus and species. Any thorough consideration of human communication needs a book of its own, so I invite you to contemplate the subject yourself. As an exercise, muse upon communication in its various forms, verbal and nonverbal. Consider the uses to which language is put: histories, sagas, myths, legends, doctrines, laws, declarations of war, peace treaties, business contracts, arguments, marriage vows, death certificates, poetry, fiction, drama, elections, confessions, blessings, curses, lectures, gossip, questions, lies, and so on.

How many languages are there within a language, how many nuances can be loaded on innocent words by metaphor, simile, irony, seduction, or paradox? What is the nature of silence in a speaking world?

An interesting meditation is the comparison of the Biblical legend of the Tower of Babel with the forbidden fruit of Eden. In both scenarios, people were, according to the narrator,

Chapter 2 :: God-Hunger and Other Forgotten Ones

attempting to usurp Divine privilege. The Tower of Babel was a building project undertaken by literalists who thought God lived in the sky, and who tried to reach His heaven physically. In Eden, the first people acquired the knowledge of good and evil, and were evicted before they could eat of the fruit of the tree of life, and thus become immortal.

"And the Lord God said: 'Behold, the man is become as one of us, to know good and evil; and now, lest he put forth his hand, and take also of the tree of life, and eat, and live forever.' Therefore the Lord God sent him forth from the garden of Eden, to till the ground from whence he was taken. So He drove out the man; and He placed at the east of the garden of Eden the cherubim, and the flaming sword which turned every way to keep the way to the tree of life." (Gen. 3:22-24).[3]

In both cases, words are essential to the story, and in both cases, God punished alleged human arrogance. Both stories also describe a fall from a more developed state of human life to a more primitive one. In Eden, an effortless life, requiring ignorance, was exchanged for a life of toil and pain as the price of knowledge. At Babel, the heaven-going tower project cost the builders a common language. The confusion of many languages destroyed work on a common goal.

"And the whole earth was of one language and of one speech. And it came to pass, as they journeyed east, that they found a plain in the land of Shinar; and they dwelt there. And they said one to another: 'Come, let us make brick, and burn them thoroughly.' And they had brick for stone, and slime had they for mortar. And they said: 'Come, let us build us a city, and a tower, with its top in heaven, and let us make us a name; lest we be scattered abroad upon the face of the whole earth.' And the Lord came down to see the city and the tower, which the

Chapter 2 :: God-Hunger and Other Forgotten Ones

children of men builded.

"And the Lord said: 'Behold, they are one people, and they have all one language; and this is what they begin to do; and now nothing will be withholden from them, which they purpose to do. Come, let us go down, and there confound their language, that they may not understand one another's speech.' So the Lord scattered them abroad from thence upon the face of all the earth; and they left off to build the city. Therefore was the name of it called Babel, because the Lord did there confound the language of all the earth; and from thence did the Lord scatter them abroad upon the face of all the earth" (Gen.:11: 1-9).[4]

With delicious irony, the narrator of each story seems to be using the hand of God to hint at wise uses of words and knowledge to attain personal and species transcendence. From Eden we learn that knowledge plus continuity constitutes divinity. If an individual lacks the immortality or longevity in which to apply knowledge to long-term projects of a material or spiritual nature, oral tradition and written history can inspire his or her colleagues and descendants to carry on the work until its completion.

The continuity of communication was disrupted at Babel, according to the story. Improvements in the technologies of travel, in the dissemination of writing, in the scholarship of translators, in audio and video broadcasting, and in the Internet have fostered a growth in continuity of communication among individuals and nations. The Cold War's space race has evolved into cooperative multinational space exploration and satellite launching projects. We've extended human presence into the heavens farther than any Babelite could imagine, for the purpose of increasing our knowledge.

The narrator of each story, with sly subversion, portrays a

Chapter 2 :: God-Hunger and Other Forgotten Ones

God somehow so fearful of human potential that He (or They) intervene(s) to prevent education and accomplishment. With a God like this, who needs a Devil?

The Forgotten One of communication depends upon and fosters the more basic instincts; it, in turn, generates and assists the instinct of curiosity. Most animals are curious about their environment, at least on the level of the edibility of new plants and animals, or of the degree of danger a new situation presents. In humans, curiosity has given rise to exploration, migration, science, technology and philosophy. When we're functioning in the mode that's standard for us, we feel an itch to find out about how things work, what they're made of, how they fit in with previous knowledge, what other people are thinking and feeling, and all manner of mysteries. It's curiosity that banishes boredom when we conclude that there must be more to life than what meets the eye–and the rest of our usual senses.

As I mentioned at the beginning of the chapter, the root of human spiritual development is a sense of ignorance about the spirit world, a hope of postmortem survival, and a fascination with the unknown. Curiosity finds better ways of doing work, of relating to other people, of improving our health and appearance, of discovering aesthetic principals in the creation of art. It pounces on scraps of evidence of the nonmaterial realms, and leads us to pursue the path of Mystery and Magick. Curiosity discovers the way of enlightened self-interest, and produces the urge to altruism, to acting for the greater good, to living and dying selflessly for the benefit of others.

The Forgotten One of altruism is subtle and powerful, and is easily masked and suspended by the more basic urges, until it manifests in majesty and might. It manifests in people who

Chapter 2 :: God-Hunger and Other Forgotten Ones

throw themselves between another person and disaster, in the bursts of super strength that allow an average person to lift an automobile from a pinned mechanic, or to restrain a vicious dog from attacking a child. It also manifests in quieter ways, in caring for an elderly or sick relative or friend, in giving time and energy to mentor children, in donating money to worthy causes. Altruism makes heroes of ordinary people, giving them the inspiration and the means to surpass their normal abilities.

It's extremely important to inform the Forgotten One of altruism with knowledge, understanding and wisdom, since innocent and ignorant altruism can make you a victim of manipulators and people in positions of authority. Telephone boiler room scams rob many an innocent altruist with phony charities and causes. Politicians and armed forces recruiters convince young people that serving in the military lets them protect their country when their sacrifices are taken for mere political ends. Informed altruism knows how to spot fake causes and victims, and it knows how to judge circumstances. It knows when to say "no" to requests for help, and it has no qualms about playing the Trickster when a person deserves or requires it. An informed altruism is less likely to develop into tyranny-by-largesse.

Altruism and our DNA understand and appreciate each other; this Forgotten One leads us to surpass ourselves, to expand our definition of "self", to transcend our present common consciousness, to achieve the next level of complexity and intelligence. It's the third power and state of transformation, and it rallies the simpler instincts to its service and to the service of our natural urge toward Mystery, the Forgotten One I call God-Hunger.

One of the "Maxims of Maat" that condensed from years

Chapter 2 :: God-Hunger and Other Forgotten Ones

of working her Magick is: "All that is, lives; all that lives is intelligent." From our Singularity, onward and outward, the matter-energy of our space-time continuum exhibits a tendency to form attachments in itself in certain patterns that are governed by inherent laws. Not surprisingly, our minds work in the same patterns we observe in the universe around us, enabling us to comprehend what we sense and to predict the course of familiar events.

If you live with pets or other animals, you know that their thoughts and emotions closely resemble our own; plants respond to kind words and good music. I've had dogs who plotted mischief, then feigned innocence when their plans were foiled; I've lived with cats who became embarrassed if they'd missed a planned landing after a leap, then studiously groomed themselves to save face. The plants I talk and sing to in the garden seem to thrive better than the ones I tend silently in a brooding mood. Large old trees offer consolation and calm in the slow pulsations of life just under the bark of their trunks.

Woods and hills, rivers and caves, mountains and oceans all have a sentience that we can recognize and participate in if we're quiet enough, and paying attention. The elegance of physical laws, the kinship we recognize with all forms of life, the wonder of stars in their galaxies and clusters, all share what I call the universal pattern of consciousness, or UPC. This pattern is based on the tendency for simplicity to seek complexity, and on the forces that arise from the relationships of parts in a whole.

Thoughtful people are usually appreciative of intelligent conversation, and they likewise seek learning opportunities and the variety offered by minds different from their own. This is the UPC manifesting both on the individual level and on the

Chapter 2 :: God-Hunger and Other Forgotten Ones

species level. Such conversations depend on shared language, standardized education and similar experiences. Universities and pubs are institutions we support for the situations they provide for such conversations. We read books, attend lectures, dig up archaeological sites, and build telescopes in order to comprehend and share with each other a more detailed map of the cosmos we inhabit.

If we pay attention to what we do and experience, it gradually dawns on us that we're missing much of the truth that the universe holds by restricting our conversations to those with human beings. We begin looking for the "Other", for an entity able and willing to communicate to us truths that we've not been able to find by our own efforts. We tend to clothe such an entity with characteristics we remember from previous sources of information: parents, teachers, older siblings and friends, professional experts like doctors and lawyers, and "authorities" of various kinds.

This characterization of that with which we seek connection has produced the image of God or gods in the form of omnipotent parents, and other authorities of lore and expertise. If we're ever to recognize the Other when we meet it, we must shatter the human images we thrust upon it. Like an only child raised in isolation, we are obsessively self-referential and we labor under the impression that we're the "crown of creation". Mystery assures us that we're not, and our Deep Mind weaves from our other Forgotten Ones the urge to pursue Mystery, the urge of God-hunger.

From the most primitive of the urges, we know that what we eat or learn about is other than ourselves, and in our consuming of it, we make part of it part of us. From sexual desire, we long to unite with that which is not us but is similar

Chapter 2 :: God-Hunger and Other Forgotten Ones

enough to us in intelligence and structure of mind that we can perceive and understand it. From flight-or-fight, we are sensitive to the unknown and conclude that ignorance is not bliss; knowledge of surrounding terrain and of any distant danger is needed for survival. From clanning, we are drawn to relate with intelligence as an entity as well as a quality inherent in the world as we see it. Clanning also encourages a learning attitude on our part, an attitude of childlike open-mindedness necessary for the contact we desire.

From the Forgotten One of communication comes the urge to pray, to call to the greater intelligence for its presence. This instinct also prompts us to listen as well as to speak, to receive information as well as to give it. Curiosity sends our inner senses questing after the divine intelligence and looking for the larger pattern into which the complex pieces of truth we have may fit. Altruism surmises that the essence of the great consciousness inherent in the cosmos, which leaves traces of its pattern everywhere, is the highest good, and thus the most desirable thing to seek and serve.

Perhaps the strongest part of the Forgotten One of God-hunger is the fact that the universal pattern of consciousness inheres in every particle of our bodies, in the manner in which those particles are arranged and linked to each other, and thus in the formation of our thoughts and desires. We are each an expression of the very thing we seek.

What can you do with these considerations beyond recognizing and learning from the wisdom of our instincts? You can file them with the information you've gained from your other forays into self-knowledge. You can alter your behavior, your reactions and your decisions in the light of knowing the strength and pervasiveness of instincts. You can discover how

they often trick you into believing that you're acting rationally or intuitively while you're following their dictates. With due contemplation, knowing your Forgotten Ones well can give you a new appreciation of civilization, custom, and child-rearing as means for imposing informed Will upon the reactions of body and mind.

Practicum: Chakra Activation

I found that the Forgotten Ones link rather neatly with the traditional major Chakras, or energy nodes, of the human body. If these nodes are open, active and balanced, recognition of and control over our Forgotten Ones are faster and more complete. This recognition and control is necessary if we are to act according to will rather than to natural instinct. It's also necessary if we want to see clearly in our visions. This is only one way of considering the patterns of human energy mapping. If you can develop your own way of seeing our neuroauric system(s), you owe it to yourself and to your fellow humans to use it and present it publicly.

Open, active and balanced Chakras invite the rise of Kundalini, a spinal energy often termed a firesnake, that empowers you with an increase of the force of the universe flowing through you (prana).

There's a type of positive feedback that draws the Kundalini up the spine through activated Chakras, while the presence and the passage of the Kundalini floods each Chakra with the force to blaze with radiance and to spin. As the Chakras are activated in sequence and as the Kundalini rises through them, you gain mastery over the qualities and powers each Chakra and its associated instinct/Forgotten One represent.

Chapter 2 :: God-Hunger and Other Forgotten Ones

The same basic technique/practice/ritual applies to each Chakra.

Enter your Temple, seat yourself comfortably, and close your eyes. Quiet your mind and your breathing through mantra meditation (see Chapter 8). From your inner stillness, when your calm is unbroken, become aware of your spinal column, of the sparkling waves of electricity moving up and down it, waves that move from and to it along the branching nerves that emerge between your vertebrae. At the bottom of your spinal column, envision your Kundalini as a flaming serpent coiled three and a half times about a rounded column of black stone.

As you gaze at your spine, you notice areas of it that glow and pulsate stronger and more intensely than other areas. You see that there are five of these nodes along your spinal cord, one at the front of your brain, one at the back, and one hovering above your brain. Step into your vision and assume the point of view first of the Chakra that you're currently working on, and then of the firesnake in its coiled position at your coccyx/tailbone; you probably will find your viewpoint shifting from Chakra to Kundalini and back throughout the exercise.

In the Chakra, feel the radiance and warmth streaming from it and spreading life-force throughout your body. Traditionally, the Chakras are depicted as lotus blossoms, perhaps because they release their energies in what appear to be discrete beams curved by the rotation of the central sphere. Call to mind the instinct associated with the Chakra, remembering occasions when you'd experienced its operation. In the firesnake, focus your attention on the heart of the Chakra's radiance, feel its attraction, and allow yourself to move toward it. From the Chakra, focus your attention on the eyes of the Kundalini serpent, feeling its attraction; call to it and open yourself to it.

Chapter 2 :: God-Hunger and Other Forgotten Ones

You will come to notice that the simple act of paying attention to the energy nexus of a Chakra is enough to increase its radiance and rhythm; calm regard focused on Kundalini is enough to stir it to motion.

The rapture of the union of Kundalini with Chakra is such that it opens a free passage in the Chakra through which the Kundalini ascends to the Chakras above it. Since its tail is rooted firmly in the tail of the spinal cord, Kundalini extends itself in length as it rises, like a string through the "beads" of the Chakras. This process takes some time to complete, both for the individual Chakras and for the attainment of full activation of them from tail to top. The rate of your progress depends on your individual diligence, imagination and understanding; some Chakras may require more work and time than others. Some may require only a week or two, others may take months. A sense of completion, understanding and power in a particular Chakra is your signal to begin work on the next one.

Leave the serpent-energy within the Chakra you've been working on. End each session by withdrawing your attention from the spinal vision, noticing your breathing, your bodily position, and the information arriving through your physical senses. Stretch slowly and touch your hands to the floor to earth yourself, then leave the Temple. When you hold your next session, begin with the Kundalini in its base position, calling it up through its channel to the Chakra you're working on and energizing the Chakras it passes through on its way.

As each Chakra is fully activated, you should notice that life presents you with situations in which to employ its power. You should also notice an improvement in your spiritual and mental clarity, as well as a greater sense of well-being and physical health.

Chapter 2 :: God-Hunger and Other Forgotten Ones

I've arranged the order of work and the correspondences among the Forgotten Ones/instincts, the Chakras, locations, and powers into a chart for your convenience:

#	Instinct	Chakra	Location	Powers
1	hunger	Muladhara	perineum	stability, learning
2	sex	Svadhisthana	genitals	allure, fascination
3	fight-or-flight	Manipura	navel	command, speed
4	clanning	Anahata	heart	bonding, love
5	speech	Vishuda	throat	communication
6	curiosity	Ajna	forehead	discernment
7	God-hunger	Sahasrara	above skull	transcendence
8	altruism	Bindu	back of head	compassion

It's wise to keep a record of your work in your spiritual journal, including a daily report of events that you judge to be connected with the activation of each Chakra. Also record the details of each session and the insights they produce.

Notes:
1. Charles Fort, *The Complete Book of Charles Fort* (New York: Dover Publications, 1975).
2. Dr. Kenneth A. Kress, *Parapsychology in Intelligence: A Personal Review and Conclusions*, Studies in Intelligence (CIA, 1977).
  Website: www.parascope.com/ds/articles/parapsychologyDoc.htm
3. *The Holy Scriptures* (Philadelphia: The Jewish Publication Society of America, 1955).
4. Ibid.

Chapter 3

Cosmophilia

The Mystery of existence draws us to experience it, to comprehend and understand it; in this effort, science and technology are excellent vehicles for our explorations. The more we know about the physical level of existence, the more accurate our perceptions and insights about the non-material realms are likely to be.

In the lands of Western civilization, the memory of Galileo reminds us of the difficulties raised by scientific observations and conclusions when they contradict established doctrines and beliefs. Even today, biblical literalists insist that Creationism is a science and that the evolution of species is "only a theory."

Blind and dogged belief in any Holy Book as the source of truth on all levels of being, including the physical level, leads to spiritual paralysis and immobility in the believer. Most of us are spiritually lazy to begin with, and any creed which promises salvation plus all the answers in exchange for unquestioning loyalty appears to be the perfect deal. It's well to remember that the facts in the Holy Books of the West are those of casual observation by unaided senses mixed with poetic metaphor and the traditional embroidery of the storytellers of the Middle East. Divine inspiration is easy to claim and impossible to prove, as are doctrines of infallibility and absolute moral authority. Scientists keep each other relatively honest by

Chapter 3 :: Cosmophilia

means of repeatable experiments, in chemistry, biology, and in some divisions of physics, but theologians, preachers and popes only have their own, or their tradition's, interpretation of a generally accepted body of sacred scripture.

World Love

Individual experience of the Mystery allegedly enshrined in and by religious institutions is often discouraged by those institutions. Teresa of Ávila and John of the Cross, the great Carmelite Spanish mystics, were considered troublemakers by the Church; whether this opinion was generated by their writings of their visions, or by their efforts to reform the Carmelite Orders, is difficult to determine, but I suspect

Chapter 3 :: Cosmophilia

a portion of both. When a cannon of revelation is declared "closed", when an institution claims that all possible spiritual truth has been received and written in a distant past, then present-day adventures into the non-material realms, into the land of God, as it were, are dangerous delusions that can lead to heresy and doubt of official revelation.

Mystery belongs to anyone who can find it, and it's everywhere and anywhere. Is Mystery God? Only for those who worship Mystery's mystique; for those who prefer unity to worship, Mystery is the great lover, the light in the mirror, a pantheist cosmos whose constant mantram is *Tat Tvam Asi* : Thou art That.

What insights has science brought to the pursuit of Mystery? For the formula of Hermes Trismegistus– "As above, so below; as below, so above"–we have the principles of holography[1] as corroboration. Created by laser interference patterns in a film emulsion, a hologram has the magickal property of containing all of its information in any fraction or piece of the original film. The smaller the piece, the fuzzier the image, but the essence is present.

The idea holds true in the cosmos as we know it. Each level of organization of complexity manifests repeated (although sometimes modified) patterns. For those familiar with Chaos Science,[2] the recurrence of the basic patterns of the Mandelbrot set also express the Hermetic formula mentioned above. There is a kinship between holography, fractal geometry, and the shapes and functions of living systems in the areas of repetition, elaboration, and growth.

Wherever we look around us, with naked senses or with sophisticated instruments, we can see subpatterns and variations of the universal pattern of consciousness, and we

Chapter 3 :: Cosmophilia

resonate with it because our bodies, physical and metaphysical, are built of the same arrangements. While we explore our physical universe, we should be exploring, in parallel, those worlds arising from, and producing, the physical: the astral, mathematic, etheric, and spiritual levels of our total being.

Another model that seems to fit spiritual experience is that of electronic communication, where a signal is impressed on a carrier wave and translated to sound and image by a receiver. Different signals can be sent and received simultaneously when they're transmitted on different frequencies; a good receiver has the capacity to pick up a wide range of signals. Our individuality can be compared to a single frequency, and our informational messages on all levels are broadcast to the cosmos. We share information with other frequencies, but our signals are unique.

There are a number of metaphors for individuality and personhood that can be found in nature. This isn't surprising, since so much of human existence echoes, reflects, and complements itself in various phases of the natural world. It's well to remember, however, that none of us are completely familiar with the marvels of our own planet, let alone acquainted with those of other planets and systems. When our quest for Mystery leads us into strange places, in "impossible" realms of alien, faerie, sometimes nightmarish images, sounds, emotions and experience, we can orient ourselves by finding the patterns of the places; there will be enough familiarity in them for us to recognize.

In the past, spiritual writers would caution the seeker against the perils of "the world, the flesh, and the devil". This deadly trio would lead a person into sin as well as distract him or her from the pursuit of God. The "world" in this case

Chapter 3 :: Cosmophilia

most often referred to human doings and interests rather than the world of nature, but many times the natural world was included in the warning. Matter in general was somehow corrupt, even though all creation was held to have come from the hand of God. The flesh signified sexual desire–or any sensuous involvement–and the devil seems to indicate curiosity and independent thought.

In my early years I held to this Manichean philosophy, and attempted asceticisms worthy of the strictest monastic practice. The internal warfare generated by attempting to live up to such antimaterial, truly stupid standards caused no end of trouble and grief. It's difficult to imagine that anyone in the last decade of the Twentieth Century would be making similar mistakes, but if you are, I urge you to cease and desist immediately; there is no virtue in pain, except in its function of warning of damage.

This is a beautiful universe. There's great elegance in the shape and motion of things, in the colors and songs and scents of this planet of ours, in the grandeur of the night sky, in the dance of quanta, atoms and molecules. Within our own species, the comedy of tragedy and the tragedy of comedy play out endlessly in extremes of virtue and vice, hope and despair. As individuals, we see ourselves differently every day, as audience, players and critics of our own state of soul. Lifetimes are limited, and we are our own judges; are we wasting time on stupidity, or are we ever seeking a greater comprehension of truth?

Questions of purpose arise: what are we made for, as individuals and as a species? Do we have a function in the great scheme of things, or are we just a fluke of nature, gifted or cursed with a type of intelligence different, as far as we know, from other types of intelligence on our planet? If we choose to

Chapter 3 :: Cosmophilia

think that we're an accident, a fluke, and then proceed to define our own function and intent, can we assume that such a choice is not programmed into us? We generally live for less than a century; is this fair, when there's more to learn than such a short lifetime can hold?

We ask these things of the universe and of each other; some of us address directly the intelligence that inheres in all things, and call it God. Truth lives in all levels of density, and to find answers, we need to explore it all and constantly question our conclusions and assumptions. The cosmos we live in is good, it is beautiful, and we and it can merge identities whenever we choose to do so. In fact, the self and the cosmos are fundamentally identical; what Mystery reveals to us is that we, other people, buildings, trees, animals, planets and stars are temporary condensations or whirls in the stuff of existence.

We need the maximum attainable width and depth of comprehension of the variety of phenomena that the cosmos holds in order to know our own selves. We do this in a number of ways, including direct observation, studying photographs, reading about things, and listening to what other people report to us. We have little choice about trusting our own senses to tell us the truth about our surrounding environment; we can ask other people to verify our observations and impressions, but as a general rule in ordinary circumstances, "seeing is believing." Our trust in our own senses shouldn't be blind or absolute, however, since disease, delirium, and hallucinogenic drugs can distort sensory signals, hiding what's there in our physical surround, and creating images of things that aren't there.

It's wise to maintain a small amount of skepticism about what we sense directly or with instruments; this is also known as keeping an open mind. Truth/Maat has more levels than

Chapter 3 :: Cosmophilia

that of perception, although perception is basic to the further elaborations of consciousness that the pursuit of Mystery brings. In the way of Mystery, the formula or watchword for the sensory level of truth is "trust, but verify."

With photographs, x-ray films, seismograph records, etc., we assume that the data they contain have not been altered in any way by other people or by environmental disruption. The fact that there are ways to alter records introduces a slightly greater amount of skepticism about their truth than we have with our own senses. One way of verifying a record of a thing or event is to compare it with other records, if available, of the same event.

A third degree of skepticism applies to the written word. A relatively recent human invention, writing and reading still carry an aura of magick and mystery that was generated when only a few individuals could practice those activities. Some people are overly ready to accept as true anything they see in print, while other people are just as ready to take advantage of this credulity.

Some scientists *have* fudged experimental and observational data to fit pet theories, or to disprove the theories of rivals, but the scientific principle of the repeatable experiment tends to keep most scientists honest. Likewise, competition in the news industry, as well as the threat of lawsuits, tend to keep most reporters from inventing "facts" that can be disproved by their competitors.

Scientific texts and research papers, as well as "straight" news stories can be granted, in general, a little more trust than editorials and persuasive essays. These latter deal in opinion and emotion, of course, and their truths (or falsehoods) are of a different order than are those of science.

Fiction's truth quotient is of a different type than is that of plain reporting. In fiction, internal consistency and evidence of a thorough understanding of human nature constitute truth. The most trustworthy form of writing is poetry, but only if the reader recognizes it as being poetry.

Writings from the past that are presently regarded as Holy Books provide a particular challenge to the seeker of Mystery. Even the purest channelings from the Akashic record, or Deep Mind, are translated into words by individuals who impart to them the characteristics of a unique set of experiences, temper, education and belief. The content of channeled truths is difficult to separate from the form it appears in and through, and individual crotchets and attitudes are sometimes taken as indicators of the nature of God, Allah, or the Buddha, etc.

The direct writings of a prophet, saint, seer, or divine avatar require a fourth level of skepticism; where disciples collect and write the sayings of a Master, a fifth level is needed.

All this skepticism seems stiff and unwarranted in the search for the truth of Mystery, and indeed much of it can be disregarded if you've developed the ability to know how to interpret the forms in which information arrives in your awareness. Do you recognize multi-layered metaphors when you meet them? Can you speak poetry? How large and rich is your vocabulary of symbols?

In our present phase of evolutionary development, humans still rely on words to communicate with each other, and words without body language, facial expression, and intonation often lack necessary nuance on the printed page. It's a good idea, when absorbing information about Mystery, to close your eyes, to silently repeat the sentence or line you've just read or heard, without any mental commentary, and to let it sink through

Chapter 3 :: Cosmophilia

your waking consciousness into your Deep Mind.

Whenever possible, spend time alone under the clear night sky; let the stars pull your spirit up and out toward the deeps of space. If you listen in stillness, you may hear the chiming and ringing of the stars, each one vibrating at its own set of frequencies against the background song of hydrogen. Feel the atoms of your flesh yearn for their starry homes of aeons past, singing in the rain of ancient light from distant galaxies.

This is both our home and self, this boundless range of space and stars; vast forces rage and swirl beyond us, delicate bits of life that we are at the bottom of our ocean atmosphere. Everywhere we look we see intricate and complex forms interacting, arising for a while, then returning to components, changing, growing, dissolving, making beauty. How fortunate we are to experience what we call the material world, to be in it and of it, and at the same time know that soon we also will dissolve into the intelligence from which we arise.

Notes:
1. See also Michael Talbot's book called *The Holographic Universe* for further information.
2. See also James Gleick's book called *Chaos: Making a New Science* for further information.

CHAPTER 4

MAAT MAGICK

As I mentioned in the beginning of this book, Mystery is the other side of Magick. It follows that the converse is true, and that both are the two sides of the same coin, as it were. In Western esoteric tradition, Mystery can be seen as a serpent twining up the Tree of Life, following the paths that connect the Sephiroth, or spheres. Magick is the lightning-flash that brings down the Promethean fire of enlightenment through the Sephiroth to ground itself in the sphere of Malkuth, in which the physical universe unfolds.

From another viewpoint, Magick is the serpent that laboriously climbs the Tree, providing experience through rituals and their results, and Mystery is the lightning-flash of revelation that is triggered by the understanding of experiences in their larger context, stunning and often destroying our "usual" state of consciousness.

Enlightenment provides understanding of existence; it comes in many levels, or layers, of reality, so that yesterday's truths are revealed to be partial, incomplete, and useful only in the limited ranges that we inhabited before we "learned better." The practice of Magick builds upon successive levels of understanding, which is why the Will according to which Magick causes change to occur is constantly changing in its objectives or goals. By its very open-endedness, Magick leads to

Mystery in a most immediate and clear way. Unlike doctrines of belief and the rationality of conventional thinking, doing Magick brings direct experience of Mystery, unmediated by other people's interpretations and expectations.

Conventional thinking isn't thinking at all, but a collection of cliches and opinions gathered from parental pronouncements, standardized classroom textbooks and teachers' attitudes, and the audiovisual input from pulpit, mass media, and friends of like mind. The net effect of conventional thinking's acceptance of dubious "truths" is a blocking of the idea of Mystery and of its pursuit. Conventional thinking is a lazy mind's way of just getting by, of buying into the propaganda presented to it by those who discourage original ideas and skeptical examination. Conventional thinkers are easily swayed by commercial and political advertising, by the messages of hate groups who appeal to fear and claimed superiority, and by their own disordered survival urges.

Doctrines of belief, be they religious, philosophical, scientific or aesthetic, stifle the questing and questioning mind by providing ready-made answers to problems of origins, destiny, nature and ethics. One reliable way of neutralizing the "party line" of any doctrine is to compare it with its rivals in its field of supposed competence. Another method is to increase the degree of skepticism with which you hear statements from any individual or group that claims to have the ultimate or exclusive truth by the same degree of insistence with which the claims are made.

Magick and Mystery must be approached with a clean mind and spirit, free of prepackaged thought, unquestioned assumptions and the non-ideas that "everybody knows". I've observed that 90% of Magick is trash removal, and that the

condition in which Mystery can be seen and understood is a new childhood, a deliberate innocence free of prejudice and expectation. Maat Magick emphasizes this new childhood in several implied and explicit ways.

Maat Magick is a new form of Western Ceremonial Magick, streamlined and simplified, and without the intermediaries common in traditional rituals, such as angelic and demonic servitors. It is ceremonial in its use of temple, altar, and Magickal weapons or tools, and it uses rituals that consist of physical movement and audible speech. It employs a number of traditional outlines of order, such as the Tree of Life, the Tarot, and the Eastern Chakra system, as different types of maps for the territory of Mystery. The performance of rituals is serious play, childlike in its intensity, and acutely embarrassing to conventional thinkers. Regular rites are guaranteed to loosen the net of ordinary consciousness and to open the self to Mystery.

In another aspect, Maat Magick is the Magick of truth. Maat is the ancient Egyptian principle of truth, justice, balance, and honesty, personified as a young woman with a feather in her headband. In the traditional Qabalistic formula of Tetragrammaton (the Yod, He', Vav, He' of the sacred name of God), Maat is daughter and youngest member of the family in which Yod is father, the first He is mother, and Vav is son. The truth which Maat embodies is Mystery itself, and her Magick is designed for its access.

Mystery is not something you receive passively and by which you are automatically transformed. The activity by which you search for Mystery and by which you use it when you comprehend it can be called Magick. Aleister Crowley named his Magickal system *Thelema*, which is Greek for

"will". As a development of Thelemic Magick, Maat Magick is also concerned with will, which is the purpose of existence. Individual will grows from the heart of Mystery and is essentially identical with it. In order for us to do our will, it's necessary to know what it is, free of the baggage of conventional thinking, emotional turmoil, and spiritual confusion.

Most of us approach Mystery and Magick with a limited, and often distorted, sense of purpose; curiosity and a desire for power are the usual first motives for searching out esoteric and occult studies and practices. Many of us live on the fringe of society to begin with because we think unconventionally and cannot accept mental and spiritual governance by consensus. We've given up the comfortable power of belonging to a majority, and we have a sense of something vast and hidden that holds the real power of existence.

We find ways of reaching states of non-ordinary consciousness, ways constructed from tradition, self-knowledge and creativity, that open doors to Mystery and guide us on how to act as we step through them. As we persist in our Magick, more of Mystery is revealed; we find our original motives to be relatively petty and silly, and entirely missing the point. We find ourselves engaged in getting rid of a lifetime's bad programming, sometimes in painful and dangerous ways.

In many aspects, Maat Magick is a "negative way", both in the sense of trash removal and in the discovery of the value of absence. If you're involved with any of the arts, or with athletics, or with any pursuit involving intense concentration, you may have noticed that you do your best work when you've disappeared, or lost your sense of self. Self-consciousness impedes the free flow of your actions, and makes the result less than satisfactory, as do any irrelevant concerns such as

thoughts of money, fame, vengeance, triumph or applause. You do your best when you're not there, when you essentially become the action rather than remaining the performer of the action. Children at play seem to lose themselves in what they're doing, and they call it having fun.

When you can disappear into what you're doing, you're doing your true will.

The three major aims of Maat Magick require and engender a childlike state of awe and wonder in the presence of Mystery; this state is innocent of censorship and prejudice, and yet it's fully aware of conditions of the "emperor's new clothes". Awe and wonder open the gates of awareness to the free flow of Mystery and its Magickal currents which empower the major tasks of willed change. These tasks, in Maat Magick, are personal transformation, taking the human race into its next stage of development, and preparing us for communication with nonhuman intelligence.

The realizations we gain of the substrate that underlies everything oblige us to order our actions and speech according to our new knowledge, and to assist, in all possible ways, other people to open their own gates of awareness. This is the essence of Magick and Mystery. Our individuality is a link in the chain of consciousness, a bridge, as it were, between the awareness of our parts and our history and the species awareness that links us with other varieties of sentient beings.

Self-knowledge includes knowing our individual place in the grand scheme of things, which enables us to expand our sense of self to include, ultimately, everything that exists, in actuality and in potentiality. The first stage of expanding the sense of self in the physical world is the development of species consciousness, in which we think and act both as individuals

and as members or units of humankind. We've been practicing double consciousness in fits and starts for millennia, in terms of family, clan, tribe, and nation.

We practice it in church, temple, and mosque, at sporting events and political rallies, at concerts, plays, Renaissance fairs, accident scenes and natural disaster sites. We experience the national level of double consciousness in wartime, at elections, and during the Olympic games. We occasionally achieve species consciousness in the face of diseases like AIDS and the Ebola virus, at the announcement of scientific breakthroughs, and in working on restoring our planet to its natural environmental balance.

It's not a large step to expand our experiences of participating in a consciousness more complex than individuality into a natural state of constant awareness. From another angle, this expansion can be seen as Jung's Racial Unconscious awakening into full species consciousness. Our underlying connection on levels of being deeper than individual consciousness is to be brought to light in everyday living in the manifestations of a telepathic web linking our entire species. The ethical concept of "enlightened self-interest", in such a state of awareness, becomes mandatory rather than optional.

Human history is not a pretty sight.

Too many of us (and even one is too many) live in disharmony and imbalance, both within the individual, with other people, and with the rest of nature. Buddha was right in naming ignorance as the root of sorrow and suffering, and the nature of this ignorance is broader than the idea of lacking facts on various subjects. The central ignorance is ignorance of Mystery; it leads to misperceptions and wrong premises for reasoning ourselves out of the painful and restricted conditions

in which we often find ourselves.

Our instincts tell us one thing and our training and society tell us something else. Science and technology have more than doubled our lifespans over the past several millennia ; what made sense to DNA's directive of continuing our species when we died at age 35 or sooner no longer makes sense when many of us live beyond 70. The hormonal and emotional imperatives of puberty urge us to mate and reproduce early and often, but the educational requirements for earning a living, currently, can make it impossible for young parents to support the children their entire beings are calling for.

Our science, both formal and informal, has permitted more of us to survive childhood and to postpone death; our growing populations cause havoc in the natural world around us as we increase areas under agriculture, housing, and shopping malls. We've killed our larger predators, and we're constantly working to defeat the viruses and bacteria that help keep our numbers down. Our practices of technologically-enhanced warfare and "ethnic cleansing" also help control parts of our population, as do inner-city crack wars and drive-by shootings with high-tech guns. The main problems with deliberate violent death is that it brutalizes the sensibilities of us all, victors, vanquished, and onlookers, and it aborts the precious work of art that is each human life.

Our Racial Unconscious is struggling to awaken from its nightmare-haunted sleep, to regain our species' sanity from its state of psychic fragmentation. Our science and technology have always been part of our nature; it's unfortunate that it has been used for harmful purpose, but it also is helping in our aim to become the healthy and happy species we deserve to be. Communication satellites in orbit, transoceanic cables,

computer-based communications networks, air transportation, etc., all contribute to individual participation in species-wide endeavors.

Our existence as a metapersonal entity hovers on the brink of manifestation, encouraged by the technological links that we're presently developing and installing. It only takes a bit of will and work in Magick to give ourselves the decisive push over that brink.

The third point of Maat Magick, that of preparation for nonhuman communications, serves to remind us that our change to a double-consciousnessed species is only the first step in the adventures that await our maturity. We share our universe with marvelous varieties of life, all of which participate in the divine intelligence that produces and supports our own minds and bodies. In order for us to be able to converse with and appreciate nonhuman life, we need to be integral and balanced within and among ourselves as humans.

We don't have to imagine the Others as arriving in interstellar craft and demanding to be taken to our leaders. Such imagery is no more accurate than seeing angels as handsome young people with wings. We already live among Others: not only are they the animals, plants and dynamic systems of our planet, but also the invisible presences that exist with us at frequencies different from our own.

There have been reports throughout history of humans encountering Others. We've attempted to describe these encounters in relatively familiar terms, so the stories arise of individuals being taken to the land of Faerie and returning to find their children aged or dead. There are tales of encounters with gods and demons, with mythical beasts and human-animal chimera, with ghostly apparitions, shape-shifters,

vampires, yeti, and aliens of various types. There are living beings elsewhere in our own galaxy and in others; the stars themselves are intelligent persons, as are clouds of dust and gas, planets, asteroids, and moons. In the substrate of consciousness from and in which the the wide and wild variety of forms arise, distance is as much an illusion as time; that which presently seems beyond our reach and knowledge is as close as our own heartbeat.

Through the pursuit of Mystery and Magick, we learn how to meet and converse with intelligence beyond the constraints of time, space, and current concepts and language. Maat Magick's basic program of individual self-knowledge, species-consciousness, and nonhuman dialogue are but beginning stages in fulfilling our purpose in being.

There are many regimens available that have been used successfully to train human beings in the true perception of reality. We continually create ourselves and our surroundings, and the great mystics of the world have attempted to tell us this in many ways, both verbally and by demonstration. Just as no description can do justice to the actuality of making love, so it is that no description of Mystery and its aspects can truly convey its realities.

I advise you to choose a system that involves all of your bodies and all your levels of awareness in the pursuit of Mystery, a system that requires your wholehearted participation and focus. Ultimately, you tailor your own methods according to the refinement and accuracy of your self knowledge; Maat Magick is simply what I've found most useful in my own work. If you are interested in investigating it as a possible example or guide for the creation of your own system of discipline, please see my book *Maat Magick: A Guide to Self-Initiation*.[1] It's a system

designed to self-destruct upon successful completion; when it works, you no longer need it.

Notes:
1. See Nema, *Maat Magick: A Guide to Self-Initiation* (York Beach, Maine: Samuel Weiser, Inc., 1995).

Chapter 5

Emotions

It's wise to prepare thoroughly for your encounters with Mystery, to clear and smooth a place for yourself to work, internally and externally. It's not mandatory that you consider yourself a Magickian or a Mystic in order to pursue Mystery, just as you're not required to belong to a religion or to a spiritual Order. It is a good idea to have some form of sacred space, a location that is private and secure, in which you feel comfortable and undisturbed.

Our emotions, or feelings, are a strong, necessary part of life, and have served us well in helping our species survive. There are times when emotions have worked to our general detriment, though, because emotions are not very wise by themselves. Emotions are psychosomatic states that arise to prepare us for action (or non-action); they work cleanly with simple thoughts and perception, but complex situations involving conflicting signals confuse them and permit them to direct our actions to often harmful ends.

A happy childhood holds few emotional difficulties, but the bodily tides of change during puberty often overwhelm us with new emotional power and strength, and with little experience in how to deal with their unaccustomed feelings. Smaller and older societies developed rituals to ease the transition from child to adult, and to teach proper behavior and community

Chapter 5 :: Emotions

expectations. In our current urban and industrial locations, we generally have lost touch with each other. Although we do form smaller societies within the larger anonymous crowd, groups like churches, clubs, associations and acquaintances arising from the proximity of neighborhood, for the most part we lack the support given to the individual by the customs and rites of shared traditions.

Good homes help prepare children for the interior and exterior tumult of adulthood, as do churches, schools and sports teams, but much of the information available to us is presented on television and by peer groups, often with confusion as a result. Western society has the bad habit of preaching one thing and practicing something else; our churches tell of the sacredness of sex, and yet television, magazine, and billboard advertisers use sexual images to sell beer, underwear, automobiles, and many other products. We have our emotions and desires tweaked in unnatural ways by marketeers, politicians, preachers, military recruiters and everyone with something to promote.

To prepare for the pursuit of Mystery, it's necessary to set your emotional house in order. First, make sure that you're physically and psychologically healthy. A major component of emotion is its glandular base; clinical depression, stress, anxiety, and any excess, lack, or imbalance among our producers of body chemistry need to be healed. If you're living with a chronic condition that you've adapted to generally, you can make allowances for its influence on your consciousness, perception and mood, and work around it.

The second thing to do is to buy a notebook and a pen, dedicate them to the service of Mystery, and write in the notebook every day, faithfully, even if to note a lack of events or results. If you want to transfer your notes to computer disk

Chapter 5 :: Emotions

from your notebook, feel free to do so, but there's no substitute for physically forming the letters of your words with your hand—unless, of course, you're paralyzed and can't use your hands.

The types of things you should track in your notebook include events during the day that aroused your emotions; what happened, what your response was at the time, what you feel while you write about it, and what your feelings tell you about yourself and your life. Another subject to be covered is your relatively long-term emotional states, such as happiness or the lack of it, falling in or being in love, rivalries, friendly or otherwise, homesickness (where appropriate), wanderlust, desires, resentments, ambitions, etc. Your notebook should also include the chronicle of your daily practice; what you did, the perceived results, and how the practice and the results affect the emotions you experience.

Such a journal, if honestly and faithfully kept, serves as a tool of discipline to reinforce the daily performance of your practice, and as a measure of progress in achieving emotional equilibrium.

A third tool for ordering the emotions is the practice of *pranayama*, the regulation of the breath. There are a number of techniques for doing this. A common one is to place your thumb and forefinger on either side of your nose, alternately closing each nostril with each breath. A breath is counted as beginning on the exhale; the duration of the inhale and exhale grows with the passage of time in a *pranayama* session, with a pause between each direction of air occurring naturally.

Your physical body should be seated comfortably in your sacred space with your eyes closed. Unfocus your mind from any particular thought or train of thought; allow any ideas or

images that arise to pass out of range without paying attention to them or struggling against them. When you feel calm and ready, begin by breathing out, and then in, through your left nostril, then do the same on your right, allowing the process to slow and deepen naturally.

A second technique that I've found useful is derived from Maat Magick, and consists of linking the breath with the four pronunciations of the word IPSOS. IPSOS is the "word of power" that was given in the reception of *Liber Pennae Praenumbra* (see Appendix A). My own interpretation of it is based on the repetition in the text of the phrase "by the same mouth." "Ipse" is Latin for "the same", and "os" is Latin for both "mouth" and "bone". In the "bone" sense, it indicates to me a deep kinship between or among people or ideas.

I don't close the nostrils for this one, but there are pauses between the inhale and the exhale that are of a duration equal to that of the breaths:

Inhale–IPSOS

Pause–IPShOS

Exhale–IPSOSh

Pause–IPShOSh

If your mental/emotional state is unusually agitated, it helps to use a mantram, or repeated word, along with your pranayam in order to give your mind something to chew on. The main point is to make your breathing slow and regular; this has the physiological effect of inducing calm and quiet in

your emotions and of persuading them to release your hostage mind. It also helps to smile.

It may seem improbable, but the bodily signs and expressions of peace can help induce the state itself. Our various functions, modes, moods, and attitudes don't live in separate compartments, but are woven together like a tartan or a tapestry. Rather than as strings of cause and effect, our moods and perceptions change as tides of influence in a field of energy. Act with or upon one aspect of the energy field, and you influence all the other aspects.

Once you've demonstrated to yourself that you can control your emotions by physical actions like pranayama, you will develop the ability to select and induce the emotions and their intensities most helpful to you in your explorations of mystery. Ascetic practices of the past erred in doing violence to the body in order to gain control of, or even to suppress, the feelings and desires that can distract the learning of Mystery. The practice of pranayama, of mantra meditation, of contemplation and reflection are effective yet gentle means of refining the emotions and subordinating them to more intelligent aspects of yourself. Tracking your experiences with emotional adjustment by writing about them in your journal assists your knowledge of your emotional body and how it affects the other aspects of your life.

When you bring your improved emotional condition into the various situations of your outer life, you may be surprised at the beneficial influence it has on other people. As they become calmer in your presence, a positive feedback loop can form that improves the collective atmosphere in which you all live and work. Your home or your office won't become a paradise of bliss, necessarily, but the general stress level can be reduced to

make life more enjoyable for all concerned.

Emotional control doesn't mean turning yourself into a robot or a statue; the state that I've found most conducive to encountering Mystery is one of alert calm and confidence, with deep inner silence. This condition requires and evokes emotions that are subtle, refined, and balanced harmoniously. Once you've quieted your agitated or painful feelings with controlled breathing, erase their shadows in your consciousness by replacing them with desirable emotions deliberately induced.

Images and music are effective for altering moods and emotions. Try visualizing ocean waves breaking on a shore, a desert sunset, a deep blue flower, a grove of willows or a snow-clad mountain range. Once you've spent enough time with an image to become relaxed and peaceful, close your eyes on the inner and just exist in the velvet dark.

In classical music, the works of J.S. Bach and of Claude Debussy are effective for me when I'm seeking calm. "Ambient" and "New Age" music, recordings from groups like Tangerine Dream, Oregon, and Deep Forest, as well as from artists like Enya and Leon Redbone, do wonders in cooling off an overheated emotional body. While this type of music is good for inducing calm, I recommend not using it during active meditation, where it would be a distraction.

There are a variety of activities on the outer that foster the subtler emotions. Taking a solitary walk in the woods, drinking herbal teas, soaking in a tub full of hot, scented water, petting a cat, contemplating French Impressionist paintings, and even shovelling snow, all help to put the worlds in perspective and to remind us that even the sharpest and most crushing emotions will pass with time.

Mood-altering medications, are, by their very nature,

artificial means of inducing calm; I lack experience with them, but I have asked friends who take them for opinions. Two people I know have experience with Prozac, for instance. The first discontinued taking it because, she said, it cut her off from the astral planes and made her feel disabled on the inner. The second one praised the drug for cutting off the voices that she'd been hearing all her life, and it also cured her arachnophobia. After listening to a number of anecdotes from various people, it seems to me that the wisdom of the use of such drugs depend on each individual's situation and need.

Most "street drugs" are not at all helpful. Methamphetamine and cocaine induce agitation; opium, morphine, and heroin dull consciousness to the point of uselessness. The casual use of hallucinogens brings a colorful and entertaining barrage of image, sound, and feeling, but it counters lucidity and coherence. Some traditions have made good use of vision-inducing substances in well-controlled ritual, but in a contemporary urban setting, its like using a sledgehammer to do a scalpel's work.

Some of our emotional turmoil arises from situations over which we have little or no short-term control, such as the death of a loved one, the breakup of a love relationship, incarceration, accidental injury, or too many bills and not enough money. With some of these instances, only the passage of time and the operation of our innate healing abilities can bring relief. In others, taking action for long-term change can, in itself, shift our emotional center of gravity into a more positive position.

As we cultivate our emotions, balancing them and refining them as we go, we become aware of the subtle interplays and nuances that underlie the more easily perceived feelings within and among ourselves. There are occasions when this emotional

refinement, in the presence of stronger, cruder energies, can make life painful. Here, too, pranayama and other methods that foster serenity can provide a buffer to soften the impact of strong emotions on you.

Your own capacity for strong emotional response is actually enhanced by refining and calming your normal emotional state; you develop a reserve of feelings, as it were, that can manifest much more powerfully and effectively when you save them for appropriate occasions. The person who blusters or weeps as a typical way of responding to the world gains little attention when an occasion arises that genuinely evokes rage or sorrow. It's somewhat like the fable of the boy who cried "Wolf!"

Serenity and confidence are conditions of soul that can and must be practiced deliberately and regularly until they become habitual if you are to perceive Mystery and to be steadfast in its pursuit. They remain in place during emotional storms that can arise and vanish during the course of a day, and can support you during more long-term sieges.

"Well begun is half done," goes the saying, and such is true in the way of Mystery. Once you begin the actual practice of preparatory disciplines, you demonstrate your sincerity to the Deep Mind and to the worlds of Mystery. The first gates unlock themselves and await your touch to swing open before you.

Peace be with you.

Chapter 6

Temple-Time and Nature

Another aspect of preparation for Mystery is the lengthening of the attention span, or the strengthening of endurance. The nature of modern life keeps us in motion during our waking hours; we have many tasks to perform in the normal course of a day. There are the things to keep our physical body happy, such as eating, drinking, eliminating, sleeping, bathing, dressing, and undressing to keep ourselves comfortable and in style. We spend time at school, at work, at recreations of various kinds, traveling between activities, and, occasionally, just staring into space.

Mystery requires that we designate an appropriate segment of daily spacetime as holy and dedicated exclusively to the quest at the beginning of our path. Just when this should be, during the day, depends on when your biological rhythms have you at your most alert; morning people should aim for a time before daily activities begin and evening people should schedule a time at night. In all cases, the physical body should be comfortable. It's a good idea to be neither hungry nor digesting a recent meal, and it helps to stretch and loosen your muscles before a session of sitting still. Your meditation seat within the temple should be comfortable for your physical body, but not sleep-inducing.

Develop a set of personal rituals for your temple time to set

Chapter 6 :: Temple-Time and Nature

the mood for Mystery. Ritual actions are symbolic, practical, or a combination of both. It's often useful to do a series of actions to help you shift gears from mundane consciousness to the lean and spare alertness that hunting Mystery needs. For example, I find that washing my hands and face before entering the temple helps me set aside the current list of concerns and annoyances I've accumulated during the day. It could work as well in the morning to cleanse your mind of the tag ends of dreams and of its automatic list of things to do that day.

In full-dress ceremonial Magick, a ritual bath with hyssop in the water is traditional; hand-washing is an abbreviated version of the same action, and serves as a good first step in setting the proper mood.

Another important step is to cut off outside interruptions in ways that depend on your living arrangements. You could lock your door, turn off the ring of your telephone, and turn down the volume control on your answering machine if you have one. Some doorbells and buzzers have a disabling switch; I used to silence a chime-style doorbell by stuffing a sock in the mechanism. Find what works for you.

If you live with other people, enlist their cooperation in having undisturbed temple time. If they refuse to cooperate, your home environment isn't healthy for you, and you should take steps to find a better place to live. If you don't have that option, use stealth and timing; schedule your dedicated time when the problem person or people are absent or asleep.

Seal your temple against nonphysical intrusion; a simple method is to walk in a circle around your chair or cushion, trailing blue astral fire that will burn in a ring until your session is finished. Another means would be to sprinkle salt or salt water around the room. If you use plain salt, be sure to

sweep it up afterward. Use your creativity to devise a method that makes sense and feels right to you.

It's helpful to light one or more candles and to burn incense. This helps to set the scene for yourself, and it also provides a bridge between the worlds of physical manifestation and the subtler realms through which you travel to Mystery. If you can arrange to have cut flowers and live plants in your temple, do so. Experienced mystics will recognize that these ritual trappings and the theory behind using them are both true and false, but they help to construct an aesthetically pleasing environment that encourages the necessary alert calm.

After you've seated yourself comfortably, go through your calming and awareness, whether it's pranayama, mantra meditation, visualization, or whatever works for you. At this point, you may find it useful to address the Deep Mind as though it were an entity separate from you. You might want to say something like, "Deep Mind, I love you and thank you for being. Show me what I need to know now, and lend me your wisdom in understanding it." Then wait in silence.

There are a number of ways for the Deep Mind to communicate with us. One resembles daydreaming in that it is in the form of moving or still images that enact and represent an occasion of interest to our progress in Mystery. Another means is a silent voice that tells us what we need to know. It forms words in our native tongue that we "hear", but it doesn't have the attributes of a physical voice, such as volume, pitch, or timbre. A third way is unlearned knowledge, which appears in our consciousness on its own, without any sensory-equivalent input. This third means carries an uncanny certainty. If it's something that requires action in the physical world, or if it bears on an important decision, investigate it before acting on it.

With practice and experience, we learn to trust, but verify. If the nature of the information prevents verification, it probably pertains to concepts that don't require action, or it doesn't apply to immediate practical decisions.

Most of us have a "critic" that passes judgment on new information, comparing it to what we already know, and running it through our processes of reason. This critic should be checked at the temple door in order to prevent it from commenting on the Deep Mind's messages to our consciousness while they're being received. Later, after the Mystery session is over, when it's time for recording the information in one's journal, the critic can be allowed to state its opinions—which are also subject to criticism by other aspects of the self.

Another way that information can be presented is through a guide or guides that appear to our mind's eye as luminous beings, as animal forms, or as religious images like Jesus, Mary, Shiva, Elijah, various goddesses, gods, devas, angels, and so on, depending on our culture, times and the beliefs with which we were reared.

Whatever the form may be in which knowledge is presented, it deserves our full attention and suspended judgment during a temple session. When the concept or concepts are complete, it's wise to remain in the state of inner silence so that the subsequent realizations can fall into place. When enough duration has passed, it becomes obvious that it's time to leave the temple. It's appropriate to thank the Deep Mind or divine intelligence as you extinguish the candles and incense, and stretch your muscles.

Record your new insights in the journal as soon as the temple session is finished. Writing is an ancient magickal and mystical tool that can create a map of the new territory

discovered in states of non-ordinary consciousness. It also allows you to compare and contrast later information with present knowledge, and it acts as a spiritual snapshot of your level of understanding at the time of writing.

It's important to the comprehension of Mystery to have access to a location outdoors where privacy is relatively certain in terms of sight and sound. If you live in a city, investigate its larger parks; if you live in the country, explore your own land and nearby state parks. If you have the time and the means of transportation, venture out of the city to a state park or to private land owned by an understanding friend.

While it's true that the entire earth is holy, there are some specific sites where power seems to concentrate itself, where the location emanates an aura of elemental energy, where the veil between the worlds seems especially thin. Take the time to find such a place if it's available in your area. Many times, these power spots have some sort of ancient structure built by our predecessors, be it earthworks, henge, or barrow of stone, or ruins of temple or shrine.

In other cases, dramatic natural features mark the spot; caves, waterfalls, mountains, rivers, and so on often are places of power. Sometimes an average-looking location in a wood or forest lets you know that it, too, is a potential gateway to spirit, and it is here that you should spend your time outdoors.

If you're entirely insulated from the natural world by asphalt, cement, and glass, obtain as many potted plants as you can support, and set up windowsill gardens, especially in your temple. Green growing things can provide some shielding from the clamor of too many human auras in close proximity. Being alone in the woods, at a shore, or on a mountain is the best situation, as it clarifies for the inner vision the Mystery that

Chapter 6 :: Temple-Time and Nature

surrounds us and that we surround as well.

City living requires two kinds of contact with the natural world: the first is daily time spent close to home in the back yard or at a neighborhood park; the second is a less-frequent venture to larger, more distant parks and power spots. There are certain days of the year when the universal current of Mystery reveals itself more intensely, days when it would be most advantageous to be in a remote location. These are the equinoxes, the solstices, and nights of the full moon.

It's not difficult to modify temple practices to fit an outdoor location; a blanket and a bottle of water are useful to have for necessary comfort. In the colder months, it helps to do walking meditations instead of sitting still. It's also good to know what poison ivy looks like, to make free use of ultraviolet screening creams and insect repellent, and to avoid the woods in tick season in the warmer months. A little practice with trial-and-error learning provides competence and confidence in being in the natural world.

If at all possible, camp overnight; even if the sky is cloudy, the ambiance of a place at night is deep and powerful, and provides a type of Mystery connection different from what you would experience during the day. If the sky is clear and free from light pollution, expect a breathtaking experience of "falling up" into the stars and merging with the universe.

This form of rapture opens you to the Deep Mind, to the intelligence that underlies everything, but only if you plunge ahead into the state, and not hold back to admire the scenery or to negotiate for continued existence. Let go; your physical body will oversee your reassembly later.

With enough practice and experience, you'll be able to achieve the inner silence that your temple and the natural world

help you to find in the beginning, no matter where your body is at the time. Churches, chapels, and meditation rooms belonging to various religious denominations can do in a pinch; people are unlikely to bother you if they think that you're praying, and the tenets of the particular religion that operates such a place have no effect or bearing on your own spiritual practice.

It's wise to retire to the inner silence at least once a day, and more often if possible. You don't have to be seeking information from Mystery. Just being in the place where it dwells (or, more accurately, in the place where you dwell with it), refreshes and strengthens your whole being. If you're in the midst of dealing with a crisis, when the opportunity presents itself, go within. The temple you create and the natural world around you teach you how to find your gateways to the Deep Mind at any time and in any circumstance.

Practicum: Banishing

The purpose of a banishing is to clear an area from psychic and spiritual interference. This interference can resemble static in radio or television reception, in that it randomizes information, rendering it meaningless. It can feel like the aura of a person or nonmaterial entity that is observing and opposing your spiritual work, similar to the sensation of being stared at in public. The interference might take the form of stress and tension from a difficult day, of a negative mood, or of memories of rudeness, spite, or general malice flung upon you unjustly.

Whatever their source or nature, interfering forces need to be removed from your holy place before you begin other practices, and also after you finish, unless you prefer to keep

Chapter 6 :: Temple-Time and Nature

your temple charged with the essence of your work.

Words to be sounded aloud, or vibrated, are italicized. "Vibrated" means pronounced with a pointed intensity, not necessarily at loud volume; the strongest emotions can be expressed in a tone of voice barely louder than a whisper.

Send your words to the indicated directions, using the body postures or actions described in regular type.

I present you with four kinds of banishments, from the simple to the complex, although many mages begin with the complex rites and find the simpler ones more useful as they gather experience. The first was developed by my husband, Lyrus.

Dragonfire Banishment

Stand facing south. As you empty your lungs as completely as possible, envision yourself as a dragon on a mission to clean and purge your designated space. As you inhale as fully and as deeply as possible, extend your right arm horizontally before you, hand straight with thumb on top. As you slowly exhale through your mouth, turn in place counterclockwise, arm and hand still extended, picturing your breath as a large plume of fire. When you return to your starting place, inhale and bring your right forefinger to your lips. Resume your human form. You should experience a feeling of quiet, cleanliness, and calm.

If you choose to banish after your practice is over, do the same as above, only turning clockwise. The longer you can exhale (with a duration of at least five seconds), the stronger the banishment. Pranayama can increase your time.

Puja Banishment

When I was initiated into Ādi Nath Tantra, I learned this Hindu banishment for *puja* (devotional rites), but it can be used for clearing the area on all planes for any situation.

Facing south, clap your hands, stamp your right foot, and shout *"Phat!"* (pronounced "Pud!") simultaneously. Repeat at the west, the north, and the east.

To me, this banishment feels like an explosive burst of air that takes interference energies or entities by surprise, pulverizing and dispersing them instantly.

Element Banishment

I learned this banishment as part of the ritual practice of the Circle of the Sacred Grove, Church of Pantheist Wicca. I've modified it slightly.

Place incense in the east, a candle in the south, water in the west, and salt in the north.

Take up the vessel of water and say:

Hail to thee, water, creature of ocean! Cleanse this place of all impurities.

Carry the water to the north, take up the vessel of salt, and say:

Hail to thee, salt, creature of earth! Purify this place from interference.

Chapter 6 :: Temple-Time and Nature

Take three pinches of salt, stir them into the water, then walk the boundaries of your temple in a circle, clockwise, flinging drops of the salted water outward with your fingertips until you return to the north. Return the water to the west. Go to the south, light the candle, and say:

Hail to thee, fire, creature of the sun! Enlighten this place from the spirit of confusion.

Carry the candle to the east, light the incense from it, and say:

Hail to thee, incense, creature of air! Sweeten this place to bless its cleanliness.

Take up the incense and walk the boundaries of your temple, again clockwise, moving the incense in small circles as you go, until you return to the east. Return the candle to the south.

I find that the tactile element of handling things in this banishment and the activity of walking the boundaries provide me with an extra measure of comfort and well-being.

The banishing rite that follows was developed in the practice of Maat Magick. It requires no instruments, such as wand or sword, and it clears interference from the intended area not only in space, but also in time. It uses the names of certain *neters*, or principles, from the ancient Egyptian pantheon.

Bes is the bearded dwarf from the African interior. He's considered a protector of children, and is used in this banishment to represent our ancestors.

Osiris, husband of Isis and father of Horus, reigned in the land of the living until he was slain and dismembered by his

brother, Set. Isis gathered the fourteen parts of Osiris, restored his fertility, and gave birth to Horus. Horus fought and defeated his uncle Set, and then enthroned Osiris as the ruler of the dead.

When a soul enters Osiris' hall of judgment, his or her heart is weighed against the feather of Maat, the *neter* of balance and justice. Harpocrat is the Child Horus, the lord of silence, and representative of our descendants. Osiris represents the ideas of father, fire, will, and the south. Isis symbolizes mother, water, emotions, and the west. Horus corresponds with son, air, mind, and the east. Maat denotes daughter, earth, the bodies, and north.

In addressing these god-forms, you address the forces and things they represent; your attitude is not of a supplicant, but of a director.

The Sixfold Banishment

Below

Bend your head so you address the earth below you.

Bes! Universal ancestor! Link us with the depths of space. Smallest of the gods, borderline of energy and matter, anchor us in the uncertainty of being.

Squat so that your thighs are horizontal; extend your arms horizontally to each side, and bend your elbows so that your forearms are vertical and your hands are in fists.

South

Standing erect and facing forward, say:

Osiris! Father of us all! Link us with the force of fire. Protector of your children, sire of the will to live, charge our will to change.

Cross your wrists on your chest, holding an imagined miniature shepherd's crook in your left hand and an imagined miniature grain flail in your right hand.

West

Isis! Mother of us all! Link us with the ways of water. Fierce as the tigress, subtle as the flow of ocean, flood our hearts with love.

Bend to your right, with the back of your right hand on your forehead. Your left arm is extended behind you, elbow bent, hand toward the earth.

East

Horus! Elder brother of us all! Link us with the arts of air. Liberator of your siblings, hawk-headed warrior lord, free our minds through winds of change.

Step forward, with your arms before you horizontally and your palms facing forward.

Chapter 6 :: Temple-Time and Nature

North

Maat! Elder sister of us all! Link us with the energy of earth. Dancer of the mask of balance, lady of the scales of justice, unite us in shared work.

Hold your open right hand upright, and place your left hand above it horizontally, forming a T.

Above

Harpocrat! Universal descendant! Link us with the aeons of time. Forever innocent, lord of silence, expand us in the eternal now.

Put right finger to lips.
When the main rite is finished, remove the boundaries of the ritual space by reversing the six directions.

Above

Harpocrat! Collapse the long aeons to the instant of now.
Hold time as an energy ball between your hands.

North

Maat! Compress our great planet to the essence of earth.
Hold earth as above.

East

Horus! Contain the wild winds by your art of the air.

Hold air as above.

West

Isis! Gather the waters in the hollow of your hands.
Hold water as above.

South

Osiris! Summon all flame to the force of your fire.
Hold fire as above.

Below

Bes! Draw close the boundaries of infinite space to be a small sphere in the here of this place.

Hold space as above.
Push the energies into a single sphere, compress it to about a quarter-inch diameter, then swallow it.

You can envision the volume of this banishment either as a sphere or as an octahedron. Experienced ritualists will notice that the Sixfold Banishment uses the form of the quarter calls, thus doing double duty.

For the inexperienced: in some ritual forms, preparing the sacred space includes not only a banishment per se, but also calling "Guardians of the Watchtowers" of the four major directions, with reference to their particular elements, powers, and human emotional components. "Scribing the Circle" is usually included to set an astral barrier to keep the energies and

god-forms you work with inside as well as to keep interference outside. In my opinion, in mystical work you don't need the barrier. The Watchtowers are useful for beginners to establish an earthed orientation, and to provide a sense of security while venturing beyond the physical plane.

Summary

I see banishment as an important component in the way of Mystery for beginners and for others who accept duality as a basic reality.

There are as many, if not more, banishing rites as there are banishers. The four presented here are examples of the variety available to you from books, from working directly with a group from whom you learn them, or from your own experiments and experience. Try each of the ones discussed on the previous pages, at your own pace, and note in your journal your perceptions of each one's effects. Invent your own banishments and note their results.

The ideal effects are peace, calm, cleanliness, and balance in your temple and in your body, mind, and heart. Subtle work beyond the physical plane requires prudent preparation.

Chapter 7

Inventory and Corrections

The entire body of tradition concerning the way to Mystery can be condensed into two words: know thyself.

For some, this advice, or exhortation, seems obvious and simplistic. Do we not see ourselves in the mirror every day, do we not live inside our own heads, don't we hear ourselves speak? Who else could possibly know us as well as we know ourselves? Ask any parent, spouse or co-worker, and listen to the laughter.

I remember my previous states of self-ignorance, times when I was certain I had life under control, certain that I matched the ideal image I had of myself; I also remember the initiatory events that demonstrated to me, often painfully, that I hadn't had a clue. Even after years of enlightening occasions, none of us are finished products. For as long as we live, we're in process, under construction, and being remodeled.

Certain important occasions prompt a time of soul-searching, questioning ourselves, and sorting things through. Moving into a new level of formal education, having a death in the family, getting married or divorced, having a baby, changing jobs, etc., are times when it seems appropriate to take stock of ourselves to discover what we really want to do, or what we should do, next.

There are equally important occasions on the way to

Chapter 7 :: Inventory and Corrections

Mystery, certain passages that are marked with significance. These occasions don't often coincide with outer events, and operate on no logical timetable. We'll investigate them in detail a bit later. The point is that each definite border-crossing, or gate-passing, requires a new inventory and reassessment of ourselves.

The initiatory inventory, as it were, helps us to consolidate our new knowledge, to digest and assimilate it, to integrate it into our point of view and into our life. Our general state of spiritual awareness changes daily, of course, and incremental gains in perspective enrich the texture of our current level of understanding. The major changes in Mystery's path are clear and unmistakable; it's akin to scaling a cliff and finding the ultimate ledge is a broad plateau (with further cliffs ahead).

The plateau itself needs to be explored, and the initiatory inventory should be repeated at the foot of the next set of cliffs, in order for our body of information about the plateau to be included in our knowledge and understanding.

What sort of checklist might we devise to aid us in our introspection? It would be wise to begin with our most recent initiation, including accompanying ordeals, if any. What has changed in us because of it? In what way, or ways, do we view and live in the world differently? How has the situation that gave rise to the initiation changed because of it? It's often helpful to use a familiar method of cataloging or filing experiences, a method like the Chakra system, the Qaballah's Tree of Life, the hexagrams of the I Ching, our horoscope, and so on. It's also good to let experience shape the form of its own analysis; choose your most informative method.

If you choose the Tree of Life, for example, you could categorize the different levels of your being according to its

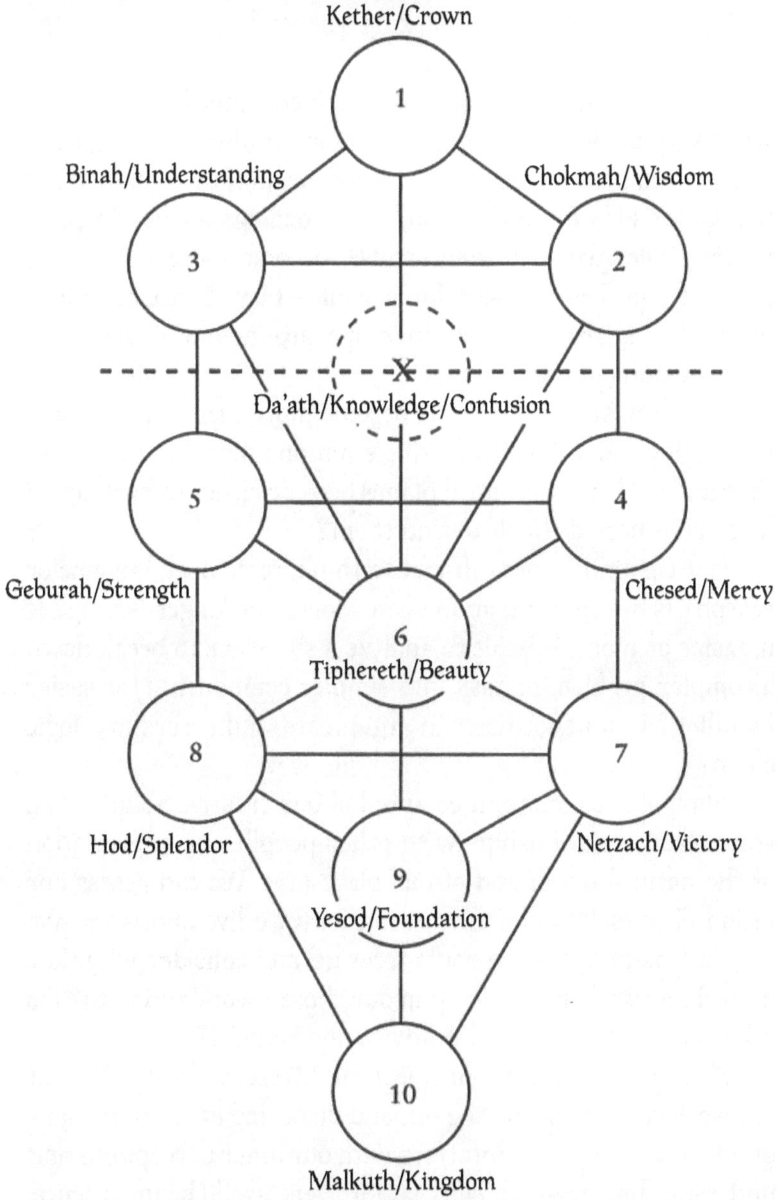

Chapter 7 :: Inventory and Corrections

Kether/Crown

Binah/Understanding   Chokmah/Wisdom

Da'ath/Knowledge/Confusion

Geburah/Strength   Chesed/Mercy

Tiphereth/Beauty

Hod/Splendor   Netzach/Victory

Yesod/Foundation

Malkuth/Kingdom

Chapter 7 :: Inventory and Corrections

design (see page 81) while asking yourself questions like the following:

Have the physical aspects of my life changed, and if so, in what way or ways? Is my health more frail or more robust? Are my finances improved, worsened, or do they remain about the same? Has my home, and/or my feelings about the place where I live, grown uncomfortable, become more relaxed, or is it the same as it's been for a while? Have I lost or gained weight? Has the familiar landscape around me changed, or have my perceptions of it?

Have my sleeping dreams become more memorable or less interesting? Are my instinctive emotions more acute, or are they duller? Have the astral planes become easier to participate in, or is it more difficult to find them?

Is it easier or more difficult to think, remember, imagine or reason? Is my concentration span shorter, or longer-lasting? Is it easier or more difficult to analyze a situation, to break down a complex problem or task into simpler components for easier handling? Can I spot flaws in arguments, and errors in a logic chain?

Similar questions can be asked of our creative abilities, the state of our relationships with other people, our appreciation of the natural world and of our place in it. We can assess our vision of ourselves and the reason why we live and work. We should look at the way people treat us, and consider why they do so. How well are we doing in our chosen work and path? Do other people seek us out for advice and counsel?

At the beginning of our quest for Mystery, the majority of the work consists of rooting out and disposing of anything in us or about us that would interfere with our inner perceptions and understanding. Some things that interfere would be impatience,

a short attention span, physical pain or discomfort, emotional distress, an undisciplined mind that pursues random concepts, or an intrusive sense of self.

Our sense of self can be imbalanced by a feeling that we are unworthy to approach Mystery, by an inflated self-importance that thinks there's nothing about us that could be improved, by a concern about the image we project of ourselves to other people or to spiritual entities. We need to disengage any sense of earning merit, or compelling fate through austerities. We have to cease identifying with our vices and our virtues, with our sins and with our martyrdoms.

Even without direct indoctrination from an established religion, we absorb the cultural values that surround us from infancy onward. Initiation teaches us to question everything that we know, or think that we know. An interesting approach to assessing our normal world-view is to imagine that we're an alien intelligence visiting Earth as a telepathic presence in the mind of a native. We can use the native's senses for observing the physical world, and use its emotional responses to stimuli for calculating its hardwired neural associations.

As an alien visitor observing a new life-form, we take note of everything about our "host", about its environment and about its interactions with others of its kind and those not of its kind. How strange are these humans in their ways of securing food, clothing, shelter, of obtaining good regard from their fellow humans, of finding love, status, wealth and the mysterious state of happiness! How odd that they fear the inevitable as well as the unknown! Some of them pursue health and longevity with a passion inspired by fear of old age and death, yet what other outcomes are there to a long life?

The existence of religion among humans seems to have

arisen from the twin needs of continuity of the self beyond death and of a comprehensible explanation of the mysteries of evil, injustice, origins, and ends. There seems to be a juvenile need, even among the adults of the species, for a divine Parent who is omnipresent and omnipotent, whose strength and wisdom exceeds their own, whose love is contingent upon good behavior, and who can punish as well as reward. As an alien observer, what can you see about your host's attitude regarding such matters?

Shifting back into your human mode, make a list of as many of the unquestioned assumptions by which you live as you can discover. Have you ever made a conscious decision to abide by the laws of the land, or, conversely, to defy and break them, selectively or otherwise? How concerned are you with what the neighbors think? How do you deal with manifestations of cruelty in small children? How dependent are you on the people you love, and they on you? What characteristics do you share with the people you know or meet, and how do you differ?

Devise more of these questions and answer them honestly, using your journal for the purpose--and include the date. It's very useful to reconsider the questions periodically in order to judge the changes, or lack of change, in your answers.

Pay attention to others' responses to you; ask people whose honesty you trust for a candid assessment of your strengths and weaknesses, areas in which you need improvement, characteristics that indicate facts about yourself. Learn to observe yourself in action, to recognize your own progress and backsliding.

Examine your desire for Mystery and your commitment to its pursuit. Do you have motives other than the pure attraction that Mystery holds for you? It's rare to have long periods of

Chapter 7 :: Inventory and Corrections

time go by without some kind of conflict or turmoil to worry about and spend time thinking about; how much do your difficulties contribute to or interfere with your quest?

What are your beliefs? What do you hold to be true about the invisible world, about God, angels, demons, spirits, ghosts, monsters, elementals, planetary intelligences, totems, allies, and all the other denizens of myth, legend, or experience? Do you see reality as a homogenous whole, or do you perceive different levels of reality? What do you consider possible or probable about matter, energy, space, time, information, ideas, inner imagery, and Magick?

In learning, we move from the known to the unknown, from the familiar to the strange. We owe it to ourselves to become familiar with the contents of our own minds and with how these contents affect our place in the universe as well as our view of it. Once we comprehend the known as well as possible, then we can see the paths and trails leading into the forest of Mystery.

CHAPTER 8

MANTRAM AND SILENCE

One of the most difficult faculties to tame and to train is the mind. It's the seat of the Ego, and is so closely linked with our sense of self that it believes it controls our lives. Much of literature and educational assumptions in the West encourage this conceit. We think of ourselves as rational animals, despite considerable evidence to the contrary; we have the capacity for reason, but history demonstrates that this capacity isn't exercised often or long enough.

Much of our action is inspired and directed by emotion. Mind avoids recognizing this, many times, by rationalizing, by claiming to itself that it had reached its own decision in an emotion-based act. Emotion is rooted in our survival instincts, and so it seems that many of our decisions and actions arise from our biological mandate to survive. The development of human mental complexity assists survival in some ways, and in other ways it seems to work against individual, genus, and environmental health.

Our present civilization, technology, economy, government and beliefs are products of mind and of minds working together. The successes of our combined thinking (and doing) have produced a situation too large and too complex for any one mind to comprehend fully. Even as the combination of curiosity and reason known as science is unveiling the workings of the

Chapter 8 :: Mantram and Silence

natural world around us at an amazing pace, the rate of growth in knowledge available to any of us generates confusion in many minds. A detailed examination of this phenomenon is available in *Future Shock* by Alvin Toffler.

Mind has a tendency to talk to itself. This can manifest as ongoing chatter framed in words and phrases, or in strings of ideas of a more visual or sometimes abstract nature. By weaving a barrier of comment and self-definition when not on the active duty of thinking, mind blocks out information arriving from "unofficial" sources, sources more rarefied and comprehensive than mind.

The pursuit of Mystery requires that mind be still. The direct approach of not thinking usually generates loops of resistance and attempted analyses of what "not thinking" consists. The approach to mental stillness that's worked best for me is mantra meditation, wherein a word with no meaning attached to it is repeated silently, with the physical body in a comfortable position and the sensory input minimized by closed eyes in a quiet surrounding.

Choose any word you like: your own name, a Word of Power, a word or phrase in an unfamiliar language, a god's or a goddess' name, a word you've received in an altered state of consciousness, or a common word in everyday use. You can render any word meaningless through constant repetition, bringing it to a condition of pure sound. When you're in the process of repeating a meaningless word, your mind will shape and change it into a variety of forms, all of which you note without denial or pursuit. The mantram can, and likely will, get louder or softer, speed up in its repetition or slow down, appear in your mind's eye in graphic form, changing from print to cursive, to a childish scrawl, or wave as though it were a

Chapter 8 :: Mantram and Silence

banner on a windy day.

Eventually, the mantram fades and dwindles, becoming quieter and more transparent; follow it with your attention, until you realize that the mantram has disappeared. Begin repeating it again, following it through the disappearance process over and over again, for the space of a half-hour, more or less. You'll find that each time you begin repeating the mantram, it begins at a quieter level, until it's the most subtle, the faintest perceptible presence that you can detect.

The state of consciousness that occurs between repeating the mantram and realizing that it's disappeared is the famous condition of no-mind. My friend, Frater Priba, describes it as the mind that's neither thinking nor sleeping. Another way of describing it is an alert stillness, in which the internal senses are quiet and open, and the mind is receptive.

Don't expect anything, or wonder what might come through; reaching the state of silence is achievement enough. What I have found, though, is that subtle awareness opens to different kinds of information, the type or types of which are suited to the work at hand or which point in a new direction. It's important to record information that appears in silence, after you've returned to ordinary consciousness enough to write or speak.

Within silence, simply observe without judgement or comment. Pay attention to the salient details of what you perceive, so that you can accurately record them later, but try not to compare the information with anything familiar to you. Sit in its presence and observe its essence, which will float around you like the stain of tea in hot water, or like the curl of smoke from an incense stick. Drink it, inhale it, take it into yourself.

Chapter 8 :: Mantram and Silence

The forms taken by the wisdom of silence draw from the verbal and visual furniture of the mind, but they can be distinguished from your "own" thoughts by an unmistakable element of the strange, the alien. Sometimes the information is framed as an image or series of images, sometimes as sounds or as spoken words, but many times it comes to you as unlearned knowledge suddenly present.

Don't try to probe or clarify what you receive in silence. When you know that you have the whole of it (and this makes itself known), keep your mind in its silent condition while you gently stretch your physical body and do whats necessary to be comfortable. Write down your new information as best you can, including any visual, verbal, tactile, musical, gustatory, or otherwise sensed, clues.

We'll return to the information learned in silence later in more detail; for the moment, it's more important to remember that such information, like anything that can be apprehended, is illusion. Much of it is tailored to your own situation and condition, though there are occasions when silence yields more valuable things.

As strange as it may seem, you're closer to the truth you pursue when the silence is unbroken by information than you are when in the white hot heat of channeling deep secrets and transcendent realizations. Paradoxically, we need the illusory information in order to attain the silence in which it comes, but while in silence, we need nothing. Progress might be measured by the lengthening of the intervals of silence while shortening the intervals of speech, which, in this case, includes all possible information.

Chapter 9

Call and Forget

One of the main tenets of Western Magick is that one must avoid the lust of result, lest it block the manifestation of your intention in the physical realm. Likewise, in the realms of Mystery, it's important to be free of anxiety and doubt. Even though the goal of the Mystic is realization and the goal of the Magickian is manifestation, both call for a detached confidence.

Humans are hard-wired to interact with other human beings; by extension, we also relate to pets, automobiles, ships, and a "Higher Power" that we cast in human semblance. Many cultures share, or have shared, the invisible world wherein live spirits, ghosts, ancestors, "Ascended Masters", angels, djinn, devas, demons, and gods. If this world were not necessary to us, it would not be with us in this age of science and reason.

The path of Mystery can be lonely, confusing and a bit frightening to a newcomer, and so it's often useful to find a guide in the invisible world. Such a guide can take many forms. In some traditions, it's an animal; in others, an ancestral spirit or god. Some seekers encounter astral teachers who exist for their duty of teaching, while others trust in wise old aliens. If the idea appeals to you, there are ways to call your guide, and other ways to determine the trustworthiness of whomever (or whatever) answers that call.

Chapter 9 :: Call and Forget

Having a guide you can trust is often helpful as you begin to explore the ways of Mystery. Like beginners in any situation, the neophytes of Mystery are awed by the glimpses of their goal that they've been granted. This awe can generate confusion and doubt, especially if you are not fully aware of, and rooted in, your own power. The company of a more experienced friend engenders confidence in the course you're following; he, she, or it presumably knows what the next step should be and how to attain it. A guide also can answer questions which are phrased properly.

You can send an astral call for the right guide for your situation. This is a matter of sitting in silence for a span, and then mentally/spiritually asking for your guide to reveal him-, her-, or itself to you. While you're at it, it's also good to ask for the wisdom to recognize your guide when it presents itself. Preconceived notions can block your recognition of that which you've called, so it's important to have a genuinely open mind.

Once you've sent out your call, go about your usual business in the confidence that it's working. The old saw, "Watched pots never boil" applies to astral calls and other metaphysical actions. Immerse your attention in that which needs to be done in your life so the incident of your call gets buried in your memory under other matters. In other words, forget that you sent out any such call. Act as though the call had already been answered, as though you already had a reliable advisor.

This means trusting the higher octave of your instincts, your intuition. Right actions and non-actions are subtly attractive, although their appeal can be eclipsed by the allure of sensory and egoistical satisfactions. When faced with decisions bearing on spiritual or Mystic matters, ask what your advisor would choose. The answer might be met with groans from your

Chapter 9 :: Call and Forget

rebel troops; this response can be a telling clue in itself.

Another case for issuing an astral call would be the pauses between events in your pursuit of Mystery. If you seem to be too caught up in physical affairs, or too bored by inner silence, keep your edge keen by calling for your next necessary set of experiences. Doing so, of course, may well unleash such "interesting times" that you'll find yourself yearning for boredom. Human beings who are drawn to Mystery are seldom, if ever, satisfied with the *status quo*, whatever that may be.

Periods of silence are necessary in the growth and life of the soul, be it silence of the self or silence of the universe of spirit. The pursuit of Mystery requires that silence be attended, that one's attention not flag from lack of stimulus, that pinpoint focus not be scattered by the random appearances of distraction. Since acquiring the ability to pay attention to Nothing takes time and practice, we are constructed to interpret events through symbolism, similarities and patterns during the breaks between silences. Events often serve to clear the spiritual air of distractions by hinting at answers, triggering revelations, framing visions and calming fears and anxieties.

As is the case when sending out an astral call for a guide, it's good to forget the call for experiences; likewise, you need to be alert to experiences that befall you on the inner planes so that you can recognize those containing the lesson or lessons you need at the time. It's a matter of cultivating your inner awareness while at the same time releasing from your attention the specific calls you send.

Forgetting sends information from the waking consciousness into the Deep Mind for processing. It's the Deep Mind that does most of the work in Initiation, as instigator and translator. Our conscious decisions, if they're resonant with the wisdom

of the Deep Mind, are set in motion by it. If our conscious decisions are not in our best interest, Deep Mind has its ways of conspiring with the universe to give us experiences that hammer the lesson home.

Practicum: Sigils

For a more concrete form of call-and-forget, I recommend the sigil method of Austin Osman Spare, an English mage and graphic artist who lived in London and died in 1956.

The materials you need are a pencil or pen, a full sheet of paper for your preparatory work, and a small square or rectangle of paper, parchment, or cigarette rolling paper without glue (you can trim off a glue strip with a scissors, if necessary).

On your worksheet, put your intention or desire into a single sentence in capital letters. For example: "OPEN TO ME, ~~DEEP MIND.~~"

Cross out the letters appearing more than once: OPEN T O M E , D EEP M I ND . This leaves the letters O, P, E, N, T, M, D and I. Put these remaining letters together in such a way that they make a design that can't be read as a word. You can turn letters upside down and backward, make some large and others small, use a stroke from one letter as part of another, and so on.

When you have achieved a design that you like, copy it on the small paper. Fold it in half and place it in a safe, but not visible, place in your temple. Go about your usual business until an occasion arises when you experience a strong emotional/physical sensation, such as anger, lust, or fear. At the peak of the emotion/sensation recall the shape and appearance of the sigil,

and send it out into the universe on the tide of your feelings.

(It may occur to you that empowering manifestations by "negative" emotions might be dangerous, but I've found that the process by which it happens seems to purge emotional content or flavor from the energies involved. An exception would be the case of a sigil created to harm another person, forgotten, and then recalled in a deliberate, self-induced frenzy of hate.)

Return to your temple, retrieve the folded paper without looking at the sigil, and destroy it. For parchment or ordinary paper, burn it or bury it. If you used the cigarette paper, you can eat it (my favorite method.) Use any method that will disintegrate the sigil and what it's drawn upon.

Your desired result should manifest relatively soon and in ways consistent with your wish. Again, I remind you that it's important to recognize its fulfillment when it occurs; keep your mind flexible and don't expect any particular form or circumstance in which it should happen.

Chapter 10

Manifestations: Signs of Progress

ften, but not always, the beginner in Mystery experiences strange events and minor miracles, unbidden and occasional. Sometimes these events are physical; at other times they can be mental, emotional and/or spiritual, or a combination of types.

A few memorable manifestations I've experienced include the appearance of a coin bearing the date of my father's death, and the abrupt sideways motion and direct fall of a potted plant "coinciding" with a gesture by Frater Priba. I've had a sofa on which I and another friend were sitting move itself several feet across the floor, and I've seen, along with a number of other people, spheres of light floating through the lower branches of a line of trees at night.

There are times when the strange events are aural, rather than visual. When inner gateways to power open, I hear a rumbling, roaring sound that begins quietly, swells to a peak, and then subsides.

My response to such manifestations is usually delight and wonder, a little thrill of confirmation, an incremental gain in confidence that I'd chosen correctly in pursuing Mystery and Magick. Advice from tradition and from the writings of elder

Chapter 10 :: Manifestations: Signs of Progress

explorers kept my enthusiasm within bounds, as it should be. Outer oddities can be a lot of fun, but they're only side effects of the essential work of self-transformation. Unfortunately, some people mistake the miracles for the essence, and trap themselves in a small and narrow place by devoting their time and energy to producing more effects.

There have been instances where people I know came unglued after witnessing a minor miracle; the juxtaposition of a seeming breach of natural law and familiar surroundings overwhelmed their mental processes to the point where they either denied what they had experienced, or renounced their practices from fear. More insidious types of reaction range from taking a strange manifestation as a sign of one's superiority to lesser beings, or as a sign of divine favor, to using such phenomena to impress followers and/or contributors.

I find it amusing, though not too surprising, that our millennial society seems as avid for miracles as the most credulous medieval mob. We seem to enjoy current technology for its usefulness and entertainment value, while at the same time we resent the "eggheads" who invented it, developed it, and sold it to us. When the face of Jesus is seen in the shadows of a water tank, or the Virgin Mary appears on a tortilla, there's a vast, unspoken "Aha!" arising from the miracle-hungry. The intellectuals may routinely produce mundane miracles, but only God can bend the rules of physics and probability–and our God can beat *your* science.

In the contemporary esoteric community, there are still a number of people who carry this attitude, although the comparison is more likely made between science and psychic power, rather than between science and God.

Minor miracles are supposed to jolt our notions of the way

Chapter 10 :: Manifestations: Signs of Progress

things are, but not to paralyze us. The inertia of the accepted holds us earthbound. Contemplation and meditation practices are designed to take us beyond our common view of the universe, but when we perform these practices with less than total attention, consensus reality seeps back into our consciousness like ground water into a ditch. If there is a purpose to miracles, it's to remind us of the illusory nature of all things.

Miracles involving inanimate objects are relatively rare; more common are the "natural" confirming synchronicities that precede or follow closely upon the discovery of a new truth. For example, when I first read about Maat and felt an immediate attraction to her, both as the personified principle of truth, justice and balance, and as the daughter principle of Tetragrammaton, I began finding feathers everywhere I went outdoors. Since the feather is Maat's particular symbol and signature, I knew I was onto something.

Other sources of synchronicities can be song titles or lyrics on the radio, topics of discussions on television, related stories or columns in the newspaper, overheard conversations in public places, a passage in a book opened at random, the questions of a child–anywhere. It could be argued that you tend to pay more attention to things relating to an important idea, but the occurrences of pointed information, in my experience, actually do increase in frequency.

There are times when you hear cogent information in conversations with a friend or a stranger. if you ask the person why he or she brought up the subject, often the response is "I don't know; it just came into my head to say it." There are times when you find yourself being the agent of synchronicity for someone else. This kind of occurrence is a type of "unlearned knowledge," which we'll discuss in the next chapter. Being

Chapter 10 :: Manifestations: Signs of Progress

someone's agent in this way affects your inner life and your pursuit of Mystery; the way in which the effects influence you depends on your senses of wonder and humor.

Direct personal agency is usually spontaneous when first experienced, I've found. Inspired words follow a rush that feels hot, electric, exciting, amazing, and sure.

During the process, I've often heard my personal censor protesting, "You don't know the truth of your words since they're beyond your experience. You could be giving this person useless or lethal information." I've learned to ignore it. There seems to be a foolproof, fail-safe factor in channeled information as it meets its intended audience. In the correct situation, the information is so on-target for the person hearing it that there are no difficulties, no seams showing, no chaff. If the person resists hearing for any reason, the information becomes garbled and pointless for the intended listener, and is quickly forgotten.

Certain professional debunkers, like "the Amazing Randi," offer large sums of money as a reward for the person who can prove (to the debunkers satisfaction, of course) that parapsychological, Magickal, or spiritual events do manifest physically sometimes. Obliviously, the "show me" attitude of such people is a powerful ward and banishment against any such phenomena occurring in their vicinity. For some reason, they hate other people's belief in things they themselves deny, as though such belief were some kind of threat.

Magickal manifestation, in my opinion, is a playful kick in the pants for the universe, tossed your way to catch your attention. To ignore miracles would be as stupid as to ignore any information. On the other hand, to worship and to become enraptured by them is to become seriously sidetracked to a dead-end path. A Magickal manifestation is a shaky platform

from which to leap to conclusions.

I've found it useful to enjoy strange manifestations when they occur while looking for their meanings and messages (if any) later. My first response to a good manifestation of the odd kind is usually a delighted laugh. I've found it detrimental to obsess about the "reality" of the miracle, or about its symbolism or meaning.

If you habitually delight in yourself and the world around you, there should be little or no problem in attaining balance in your regard and judgement of Magickal/Mystical manifestations.

Chapter 11

Unlearned Knowledge

Physical manifestations of non-physical events, entities or conditions often, but not always, accompany "progress on the Path". As I mentioned before, it's best to treat them as a matter of fact and not permit yourself too much agitation about them, whether fear and denial, greed and pursuit, pride and egoism, or any other kind of fascination.

A different kind of manifestation, that of knowledge suddenly appearing in the mind, usually provokes an "Aha!", and a marvelling at how very apt it is, as if the obvious had been abruptly unveiled.

If the unlearned knowledge urges you to act, or if it changes your mind or point of view on a person or concept, you can check it out before acting upon it or accepting a new opinion as your own. Challenge the knowledge for a word or image of validation, and analyze it through Gematria for a congruity of meaning and/or topic. My favorite resource for the purpose is *777 and Other Qabalistic Writings of Aleister Crowley*. It presents instructions and tables of correspondences needed for the purpose of analysis.

Not every occasion of unlearned knowledge will provide such means of identification, nor any certain method of testing it. You can probably trust your own considered judgement in evaluating the worth of unlearned knowledge for your

current situation. If it appears to exist in a vacuum, record it as accurately as possible for later consideration; occasionally, such information is delivered some time before it's understood or needed.

There are several kinds of knowledge that might appear to your mind's eye in the course of meditation, contemplation, or at times when you're engaged in various activities that don't demand your total attention, tasks that you do in a more or less automatic way. For instance, you could be doing laundry or washing dishes, when you're suddenly convinced that you should contact a friend or relative, with no particular message in mind. If you follow through and make a phone call, you might find that the person is dealing with a problem, and that you're able to help him or her.

This is worldly, or mundane, information, and has its place in life. There's also practical, spiritual knowledge that presents a ritual, or series of practices designed to ready you for a new way of seeing. If the suggestions are not harmful to your health, the best test of their worth lies in doing them for a long enough time for them to be effective. This type of knowledge might take the form of an urge to change your sleeping patterns to enable you to have solitude and silence at dawn, for example, or to undertake devotions to a particular godform for a set period of time.

If Mystery leads you to devotion to a divinity, you'll need to generate a total belief in that divinity for as long as the practice continues. Austin Osman Spare and contemporary Chaos Mages emphasize the practice of belief empty of content. This means that belief, which I see as a form of love, must be free of particular objects; it must be mobile, polymorphous, adaptable and swift to respond to the desire and will of the Mystic/Mage.

Chapter 11 :: Unlearned Knowledge

This opposes many religions' insistence on belief or faith as firm and unchanging; were it so, then the holders of an unchanging belief or faith would suffer tremendously, trying to remain in outgrown shells or carapaces after their spirits have explored and expanded beyond tenets and dogma. Like many other tools in the kit, belief makes a good servant but an ill master.

It's a good idea to limit devotional exercises for a particular godform to a definite period of time, be it a moon/month, a season, or a year. Another good idea is to practice devotional workings to several godforms, in series or in parallel, and to be utterly sincere with each one.

Another type of unlearned knowledge is that of cosmic or historical "facts" or events that are essentially unprovable. These can add to your sense of wonder and the general fitness of things, but they generally miss the point of self-knowledge and personal transformation.

In my own case, I've perceived the story of the "mad star near Betelgeuse" who considers planetary life, and indeed all non-stellar life, as a form of disease. It forms virulence from its own substance, encapsulates it (in a manner incomprehensible to me) as a multitude of charged units, then hurls these missiles of destruction at near light-speed toward living planets, asteroids and moons. Other, saner, stars deflect these missiles for the most part, sending them into black holes or consuming them in their own solar cores. A few get through.

The virulence inspires self-destruction; the more complex the intelligence, the more it's affected. When I discovered this scenario in my mind, it served as a temporary answer to the mystery of human stupidity, one of the great koans that engaged me at the time. I held it as literal truth for a number of

Chapter 11 :: Unlearned Knowledge

years, and it did little, if any, harm. I didn't see it as an excuse ("The woman tempted me, and I did eat."), nor as a Messianic opportunity, but as a logically-satisfying explanation of why we and the planet we inhabit are in such questionable shape. The idea leaves open the possibility of detoxification and restoration of health and balance, without requiring divine redemption and inborn guilt.

Everything's possible until you look in the box. The power of Mystery lies in its quantum-uncertainty nature, like the condition of Schrodinger's Cat. The image is that of a cat in a box equipped with a lethal gas-delivery system, which is linked to a trigger sensitive to the random decay of a nearby sample of radioactive substance. The cat is described as being 50% alive and 50% dead until the experimenters open the box and observe it. This is statistical sleight of mind, of course, but it illustrates an aspect of Mystery.

The best use I've found for such unprovable assertions of unlearned knowledge is as mental solvents, inner-life experiences that loosen the sense of "the way things are" and "everybody knows". Keeping your perception, apprehension, and conception loose and flowing, while keeping your assumptions tightly leashed, requires practice, perseverance, and occasional help from your friends.

Generally speaking, encountering unlearned knowledge often produces an astonished euphoria, a flood of wonder, an explosion of awe, particularly when it concerns the nature of consciousness itself, of the universe, and of that which is indicated by the word "God". This is a form of rapture that keeps gateways in the mind (Hod), in the emotions (Yesod), in imagination (Netzach), and in the heart (Tiphereth). Even so, this unlearned knowledge is *knowledge*, with its seat in Da'ath.

Chapter 11 :: Unlearned Knowledge

Every form of rapture carries with it the danger of its being mistaken for the supreme attainment, of which there's no such thing. The deadliest idea a Mystic/Mage can hold is that he or she "has arrived." This leads to abandoning your practices, to thinking that you are somehow better than others, to freezing in place, in stasis, in delusion. Knowledge of or about something is not the thing itself.

On the Magickal side of the coin, one of the saddest figures is the armchair Mage, the library Magickian, the clean-handed theorist. In Mystery, those who seek to prolong the trance of knowledge work to prevent their own direct experience of that which is known of, or known about. The joy of discovery is a lot like falling in love; there is a distinct spiritual pleasure in adding to our store of information, a delight at having our mind expanded, as it were, an urge to comprehend a revelation with the eagerness of a lover.

Unlearned knowledge, like any other form of knowledge, needs to be processed in contemplation, in meditation, and in just being with it in silence. You need to find the measure of the information: its territorial boundaries, the depth, or number of levels in which it's true, its extent of application, its meaning. How does it fit in with what we already know? Where is its place in the grand scheme of things, and why was it given to us at this time?

Be careful of the trap of assigning origins to unlearned knowledge. Its source is irrelevant. Impressions of grandeur do not constitute authority, nor does meaningless dismissal–"It's probably just something that your subconscious kicked out"–invalidate the worth of the information itself. Although unlearned knowledge sometimes seems to refute past opinions and experience, it's wise to consider it as a possibly "higher",

Chapter 11 :: Unlearned Knowledge

more inclusive view of its subject. This consideration can expand your view of things, can open your mind and take it beyond its present set of limitations. On the other hand, if the information doesn't produce such expansion and becomes a point of confusion, write it down and save it for later.

The four powers of the Sphinx are Know, Will, Dare, and Keep Silent. The fourth power is an especially good friend in the realm of unlearned knowledge. The exception to silence is when unlearned knowledge occurs in the course of a divination for another person. In such cases, the information is directed toward the querent and should be shared with him/her. I've found that during a Tarot reading I often feel a hot rush of certainty and a sense of elevation as I speak about the meaning of the cards; the words I hear myself speaking in this condition are usually rooted in the conventional meanings but go beyond them, often to a considerable distance.

In cases of spontaneous knowledge that applies generally, or that presents itself as a universal truth, keep it to yourself and, possibly, a trusted advisor. If you have a teaching relationship with other people, there's a great danger in telling them of it; it could be taken as prophecy and accepted as proof of your holiness or inerrancy. Even if you think that such a situation could accelerate the initiatory progress of your younger colleagues, resist. It could trigger a "cult of personality" centered on you, it could establish a fixed belief in the minds of your colleagues, and in yourself, and it could instigate huge ego problems in them and in you.

Your journal/record/diary is the place for unlearned knowledge until such time that you've proved its truth to the satisfaction of your mind, soul, and heart.

In addition to the unlearned knowledge revealed through

Chapter 11 :: Unlearned Knowledge

divination and spontaneous trances of various kinds, there sometimes occurs knowledge after rapturous visions/experiences. It's as though the "raptor" presented you with a precious egg for incubation.

This type of knowledge is the most difficult to frame in words since it's shaped to your own measure. Its general sense is that of "All is well, as it was, is, and ever will be." It pervades all levels of your being, remains with you for a considerable length of time, and it "hatches" slowly as a luminous mist that's only gradually obscured by the daily routine of living. Remembering the rapturous vision can restore the hatchling to your awareness, where you can immerse yourself in it to clear away the detritus of illusion and invite new rapture.

Silence naturally surrounds this third type of unlearned knowledge, since it's nobody's business but your own. It's not a thing to be conveyed to another in words or by any other means; it can be hinted at or pointed toward in the various arts, but the best you can do for other people is to recommend practices to ready them for their own experiences of it.

Even with the unspeakable ecstacy of rapture, the main danger is getting stuck in a closed loop with it and thinking that you've "attained". Ecstasy is a great refreshment, but it's necessary to move beyond it.

Practicum: Gematria

Gematria is a system for discovering correspondences between names and ideas through the comparison of the numerical value of letters and words. Unlike English, the letters of Hebrew carry number values; some letters have two values: one for use at the beginning or middle of a word, and a second

Chapter 11 :: Unlearned Knowledge

for use at the end of a word.

The sum of the values of the letters of a word equal the value of the word. Words that have the same number are linked to each other on various levels of meaning. It's also possible to add, subtract, multiply, and divide significant numbers with each other to yield a value for a third word.

In traditional use, vowels aren't counted in, but in the transliteration of a word from English or from any language that doesn't use its letters for numbers, I consider vowels to be valid components of meaning.

Although there are several systems of English Qaballah in existence, I have had satisfactory results with the Sepher Sephiroth section of *777 and Other Qaballistic Writings of Aleister Crowley* as a handbook, since it contains an easily read comparison of Hebrew letters, English letters and letter values. It also has an extensive list of words corresponding to a given number, arranged numerically.

Use Gematria to check the validity of visionary information. Whenever possible, while in the vision, ask for a name or a word. If necessary, ask for its spelling. As soon as you can, write the name or word in your record, then fill in the narrative and descriptions of the vision. Decipher the word into its number, then look up the number in the correspondences list. The words listed for that number should provide words that relate closely to the character, tone and content of your vision. If the words listed for that number are contradictory to the word you're testing, examine the content of the vision more closely and critically. In the end, you have to trust your own good sense concerning what to believe about anything.

As an example of how Gematria works, I'll take you through the process I used when verifying a name of a person from a

Chapter 11 :: Unlearned Knowledge

vision. First, I'll list the comparisons, including the values for the final forms of letters where applicable:

Hebrew Letters	English Equivalents	Values (* = finals)
Alef	A	1
Bet	B	2
Gimel	G	3
Dalet	D	4
Heh	H (E)	5
Vau	V (U)	6
Zayin	Z	7
Chet	Ch	8
Tet	T	9
Yod	Y (I or J)	10
Kaf	K	20 500*
Lamed	L	30
Mem	M	40 600*
Nun	N	50 700*
Samek	S	60
Ayin	O (A'a or Ng)	70
Pe	P (F)	80 800*
Tzaddi	Tz	90 900*
Qof	Q	100
Resh	R	200

Chapter 11 :: Unlearned Knowledge

Shin	Sh	300
Tau	T	400

The vision concerned means to establish stability and a place of one's own in the astral planes. The person in the vision, who was levitating great blocks of sandstone and fitting them together as a structure, named himself Hymnot, Dream Master of Tarion. He was robed in gray, had white hair and beard, wore a black laurel wreath on his head, a black symbol of Saturn around his neck on a chain, and carried a wand tipped by a crescent moon, all in black.

From him I learned the principles of establishing a home/temple in the astral planes; he demonstrated that anything imaginable can be built there. Just to verify the internal cohesion of the vision, the person, and the idea of an astral temple, I decided to analyze his name with Gematria. I gave the "O" in his name its value of 70.

I sat down with paper, pencil, and my copy of 777, first listing the letters in the name, with their number values beside them as follows:

```
H =  5
Y = 10
M = 40
N = 50
O = 70
T =  9
   ___
   184
```

I then referred to *Sefer Sephiroth* to check on the words or phrases associated with 184, which were "Ancient times;

Chapter 11 :: Unlearned Knowledge

eastward". I considered this congruent, since Saturn, whose symbol hung around Hymnot's neck, is, in turn, a symbol for time and age. "Eastward" didn't seem especially significant, except that east is where the sun rises to begin a new day, and days are a measure of time.

In experimenting with 184, I found that 184 divided by 8 yielded 23. Words with the value of 23 include "parted, moved, separated; joy; a thread; life." Words with the value of 8 include "to will, intend; entrance, threshold". "Joy" isn't an attribute often associated with somber Saturn, but in the vision, he seemed to be enjoying his work. He certainly was "parting, moving and separating" the sandstone blocks before he floated them into place in his structure. The words "a thread" and "life" evoke, for me, the Fates spinning out the thread of one's life—and cutting it: another measure of time.

The words with the value of 8 also seem congruent with a Saturnian astral (Lunar) vision. "To will, intend" indicates a link with the formula of love under will, and also a firm control of one's doings and whereabouts in a misty dreamtime. "Entrance, threshold" seems to speak of a next step in the pursuit of Mystery or Magick.

It worked out well enough for me; I was satisfied with Hymnot's basic honesty, and so I proceeded to create my own astral temple, which I discuss in the next chapter.

Ease with working Gematria comes with practice; it requires a general grasp of Qaballah only earned by faithful study and application. It's not the only way to verify astral information, but in my opinion, it's the most thorough. Gematria is not a mechanical process, however. It requires your own abilities of interpretation, grasping of nuances and intuition. It's mind's way into Mystery.

Chapter 12

Astral Adventures

hen you begin the practices of meditation and contemplation, which are the most reliable physical gates to Mystery, you may find strange images in your mind's eye, hear silent sounds, and feel a chill no matter what your environmental temperature is. In meditation, the idea is to let such impressions arise and disappear without fighting them or following them, and to resume repeating the mantra, noticing breathing, or doing your chosen action to evacuate your mind of anything in particular.

In the silent consideration which is contemplation, your point or subject may begin to change its nature and/or form, sometimes in disturbing or frightening ways. A candleflame can change to an inferno, a tree can become a leafy ogre, a crystal can seem like a glacial cave, or the object of your contemplation may disappear and you find yourself regarding something else altogether.

It's possible to be doing an entirely mundane task when "otherness" surrounds you and unlikely scenes and characters intrude upon your awareness. One of the more remarkable experiences I've had of this situation occurred early in my pursuit of Mystery through Magick.

I was changing bed linens, with a pillow tucked under my chin while I pulled on the pillowcase, when I found myself facing

a white rock wall. There was a large rounded-arch opening in it, through which I saw a dim, vast space with rows of dull green humming shapes that I knew were machines of some kind. At the same time I could see the children's bedroom behind and through the wall, as though I were looking at superimposed film transparencies.

My physical body was frozen in place; I couldn't move, even to release the pillow under my chin, nor could I turn to either side to see what might be surrounding the section of wall with the opening and the green machines beyond it. I heard a male voice ask me, "Are you ready for your name?" I almost said "Yes", but I was taken by a sudden inspiration, and replied, "I choose to work nameless." "Very well," the voice responded, "then you'll be known as 'Nema'." The wall disappeared then, and I could once again move my physical body.

I recalled from my Magickal studies that "Nemo," the masculine form of the word, means no-one, and that it's the non-name of the Master of the Temple, so I use the designation to mean both "nameless" and "no-one". With some amusement I also noticed that Nema is Amen spelled backwards, and that some people might find this Satanic or blasphemous. If Amen means "so be it", then Nema, in my opinion, also means "maybe yes, maybe no, what's the difference?".

The astral planes are closest to the physical plane in their density, or tangibility, and yet they can be distractingly strange until you become familiar with them through practice, Traditionally, the astral planes are divided between upper and lower; there are further divisions, but the two major ones will do for now. The upper astral is the realm of lucid dreaming, of guided meditations, of your personal portal to the astral commons, and the realm that translates information into

Chapter 12 :: Astral Adventures

visions. The lower astral region is the territory of nightmares, of raw emotional reactions, of vampiric forces, incubi, succubi, ghosts and dead astral bodies, of the shells of creation called the Qlipoth, of madness and of hungry, half-realized desires.

When you first begin your initiatory practices, you shine like a beacon on the astral planes in your vitality and in your aspirations. This light of intelligence attracts the notice of the lower astral nasties, and they gather around you in the hope of feeding on your vitality in whatever way they can. Some of the symptoms of vitality-leeching are fatigue, distraction, confusion, foggy thinking, lack of ambition, shunning work, and spiritual stupor. To avoid these conditions, thoroughly banish the location of your meditations before and after you meditate.

Perhaps the most famous banishing rite in Western Magick is the Lesser Banishing Ritual of the Pentagram. In his book *Modern Magick,* Donald Michael Kraig explains and teaches the LBRP excellently.[1] There is a banishing rite in *Maat Magick* that's available in Chapter 22.

You may well be drawn to explore the lower astral. I've been so drawn, and so have a number of colleagues; darkness calls to darkness. Danger adds a thrill to curiosity. The rebel and the romantic seek out that which respectable folk fear and condemn, if for no other reason than that respectable folk often fear and condemn the romantic and the rebel. (If They hate it, it must be wonderful!)

The lower astral is home to Lovecraftian aliens, to the glamour of the vampire mythos, to the shadows of werewolf, ghoul, zombi and demon. It touches and mingles with the density of the physical plane in fiction, in art, in poetry and in persons who craft a Gothic look and style as a nightly mask. There's a fine line that's easy to cross between enjoying the

Chapter 12 :: Astral Adventures

tang and savor of the dark and becoming obsessed by darkness itself.

There is a stage of initiation in which you're required to explore the darknesses of both the lower and the upper astral planes, a stage marked by your integration with your essential self. Before you've established this integration, however, it's wise to avoid overexposure to lower astral locales and denizens. You need your natural vitality for the pursuit of Mystery and for the active disabusing of your own notions. If you lend yourself to vitality drain by lower astral types, you not only weaken your own constitution, but you, in turn, begin to sap the vitality of other people.

Vampirism aborts your courtship of Mystery. If you permit parasites to feed on you, you'll become a parasite yourself, abducted and locked into a chain of need and greed, robbing from others that which you should be generating. This creates a closed loop that traps you in a small corner of life and cuts your contact with Mystery. It's worth the effort to avoid, to resist and to escape lower astral situations, to rise through them to the upper astral ranges, to transcend the general astral realm cleanly and quickly.

Even though lower astral entities are relatively stupid, they do have a low cunning sufficient to fashion lures for the unwary, to appeal to kindness and pity as well as to lust and avarice.

Many years ago I spent a substantial amount of time exploring the astral planes, upper and lower. I've never seen a distinct borderline between the two realms; there's more of a zone that shares characteristics of both upper and lower natures. One day I found myself in this zone. The surround was a featureless dark gray that seemed like air or sky.

From the upper left area of vision there sailed a giant

Chapter 12 :: Astral Adventures

peapod, light tan and translucent. It had a stem on one end and the upcurved prow-shape on the other. Veins branched under the translucent skin of the pod, traced in raw sienna. Inside the pod was a man; he had dark hair, and neatly-trimmed moustache and beard. He was dressed in scarlet and gold Renaissance costume.

He pounded on the walls of the pod with his fists, his face frantic; his mouth opened to scream and speak, and I couldn't hear a sound.

When he saw me, he went down on one knee, clasped his hands, stared at me beseechingly, and gestured his desire to be free of the pod. I moved toward him with the intention to help, and almost immediately felt warned away. I argued with myself for a while, but finally decided to pay no more attention to the man or to his pod. When I wrote of this encounter to Kenneth Grant, he responded that it was good that I refused to try to aid the person; otherwise, I would have wound up inside the pod and the man would have been released. Narrow escape? Perhaps.

The upper astral can be just as entertaining as the lower astral, perhaps even more so. Its dangers differ from those of the lower astral in that it seduces through moonlight rather than through shadow. Things on the upper astral have a misty glow about them, silver, pearl, opal, amethyst, that lures curiosity, calls the dreamer, and winds a silken web around your attention. The only way to safely traverse the astral realms is to not care about outcomes, to refuse to pursue the glimpse, the faint scent, the whispered echo, to postpone wonder until you're well-earthed. It doesn't do, however, to entrench yourself in pedestrian attitudes or to anchor yourself in the density of the physical plane through a narrow definition of "reality".

Chapter 12 :: Astral Adventures

I suggest employing the nature of the astral planes to create a base for yourself, a second Temple that echoes and is linked to your physical working/sacred space. This will provide for you a refuge from intrusions and a means for directing your attention to the work at hand; it also can be a place of rest and recreation, which are also important to transformation.

Imagine/visualize a setting and a structure in that part of the astral planes that is private to you, a place I call your vestibule. Although most of the astral realm is common territory open to all sentient beings, you have an inviolate, personal area within the realm that is known only to you and to those you invite, through description, to share it. You have the power to shape anything within your vestibule. Make your Temple as simple or as complex as you will, fashioned by your own aesthetics, and in as clear an image as you can manage. If you include in its furnishings a mirror, window, pond, or other means of seeing, you provide for yourself the choice of participating in events occurring in the astral commons, or of viewing them in the privacy of your own Temple.

The astral realm has its uses. Through it and in it, you can gather information about people and events in physical reality that might not be available physically. You can meet and converse with symbols, who are living entities, astrally, to enrich your understanding of their meanings. If you develop the necessary expertise, you can locate and converse with faeriefolk, nature spirits, devas, godforms and goblins, as well as with shades of the dead and the primordial archetypes of humanity. Certain fictional characters and creatures can be found in the astral planes, those who have passed the test of time since their creation by their resonance with generations of readers.

Chapter 12 :: Astral Adventures

It's possible to reach the hall of the Akashic Record through the astral planes, although it's difficult to interpret what you find there with just a physioastral level of consciousness and awareness. The record contains, among other things, the complete history of the human race, including its forebears, and also a projection of the probability-worlds of the future. You can find the history of your particular individuality here; again, with the proper expertise, you can review your life/lives while you're still alive physically. The usual course of events has the Akashic review taking place after physical death and before astral death.

At the beginning of this chapter I mentioned dead astral bodies; we die three times in our passage out of life, shedding in turn our physical body, our astral body, and our etheric body. Other than specifying funeral arrangements before we die physically, there's not much we can do about the disposal of our physical corpse. We trust our relatives, friends, executors, the state, or Nature to do the job for us.

When we leave our astral body, we can command its dispersal into the essences of the classical elements of fire, water, air and earth. The essence of the elements are present on the astrals plane, linked to their physical manifestations. If we choose fire, we seek out a physical fire and walk into its astral presence; if water, we slip into the aura of a river, lake, or ocean and let it dissolve our astral body; if air, we find a high place and release our astral bonds, becoming like mist or cloud, blown by the winds. It's also possible to simply will the astral body to disperse in a flash of light.

If you don't see to the disposal of your astral corpse after death, it becomes a vampiric shell, swimming with other incomplete and distorted forms on the lower astral, blindly

seeking energy sources. The point of this information is to encourage you to become familiar enough with the astral planes so that you properly dispose of your remains after you die; it's the thoughtful and courteous thing to do.

While you're still alive, familiarity with the astral planes provides you with necessary portions of self-knowledge: the interpretation of symbols from the Deep Mind, learning your emotional responses to various triggers, placing the control of these responses under the dominion of will, reading the reactions of others, and more. Practice and experience let you use your astral abilities to gather certain types of information at a distance, to communicate below the level of waking consciousness with others, to diagnose and treat psychic ailments, to release ghosts and other kinds of trapped sentience, to learn the arts of preverbal persuasion.

There are many books on the market that deal with out of body experiences (OBEs), astral travel, dream interpretation, and other astral phenomena. Such things are mysterious and fascinating, but they exist on the fringes of Mystery, and can become time-wasting obsessions. In your first formal explorations of the astral planes, it's best to be as businesslike as possible: banish every time you meditate, and pass through the lower astral without tarrying, keeping detailed notes in your journal of your experiences in the upper astral regions, as well as of your interpretations of and conclusions about your visions.

You'll be returning for a thorough investigation of the lower astral realm and its denizens after you've attained acquaintance of more rarefied states of perception and consciousness.

Whatever practice you employ to reach the light trance state–drumming, chanting, dance, meditation, contemplation–

Chapter 12 :: Astral Adventures

that opens for you the astral gates, persist in it to take you through the lower astral and into the upper regions. Sometimes it's difficult to judge how much time on the astral is enough for learning its nature while avoiding its seductive glamours, but the call of greater Mystery should be sufficient for summoning you onward.

Notes:
1. Donald Michael Kraig, *Modern Magick: Eleven Lessons in the High Magickal Arts* (St. Paul, Minn.: Llewellyn Publications, 1989), 33.

Chapter 13

Cosmic Visions

Beyond the astral level of consciousness lie the twin towers of intellect and intuition. Between them stretches a type of barrier or discontinuity, like a boundary between fields of gravitational influence, a boundary that can be crossed at the central region of balance, and at either extreme. The region of balance between intellect and intuition functions as a lens, concentrating and diffusing, in varying proportions, the attracting radiance of Mystery. This radiance illumines the astral planes, and draws onward the temporarily satisfied astral explorer.

Analytical thinking and artistic creation need regular exercise in the pursuit of Mystery. Together, they're a pair of wings that are also towers as you approach them, and tools as you depart.

The intellect is a proud but limited creature, aspiring to a Theory of Everything but distracted into lint-picking. It transcended the limitation of language by discovering mathematics, yet it's only as accurate in its finished thoughts as its available data and its repertoire of logics permit. It sees no concept as being beyond its comprehension: when it encounters experiences that seem to contradict its opinions and cherished conclusions, it's swift to claim hoax or hallucination. It often mistakes itself for the self and/or the will. Trouble arises when

Chapter 13 :: Cosmic Visions

a person embraces the concept of intellect as self, and acts accordingly.

We've met the type. If the self settles into the intellect as "home", we have the nerd, the absent-minded professor, the armchair mage, the nonstop theorist. There are also those who repudiate the intellect, preferring to live in a "state of Nature" by instinct and feeling. There are also those who deride the intellect as a cultural or ethnic marker, as something effeminate, or as something totally masculine and unladylike. Each transphysical realm has its normal functions that occur as part of the Mystery we seek. To worship or to deride any of our aspects is a mistake obvious to anyone not making it.

Each realm has its shadow, its dark aspects, its hells, as it were. Those who exalt the intellect and those who renounce it share the same dark hell of self-restriction. There is information you need that often is misunderstood by the intellect, which tends to promote itself to its natural limits, and then stays there. Some intellects deny the reality of that which they can't comprehend, refusing to listen to aspects of themselves that do comprehend it.

Functioning properly, the intellect is a valuable tool/viewpoint. It analyzes well, separating and cataloging the components of a complex construct. It's good at comparing new data with old, at sorting things and events into their proper categories, and at finding patterns in seemingly random distributions.

Intellect shares the faculty of memory with other human powers. In its own segment are memories of mental things: learned facts and formulae, personal discoveries that can be framed and expressed by the mind, patterns of events and facts, hypotheses, theories, and trivia. Intellect's memory isn't

Chapter 13 :: Cosmic Visions

restricted to the normally-perceptible worlds, but includes memories of energy signals, quarks, atoms, molecules, cells, tissues, organs, systems and wholes. These memories are the bases for mind's healing abilities.

The intellect usually functions best when its gates are open to other realms for the two-way traffic of information. If left to itself for too long, without ways to inhale data, exhale conclusions and employ certain of its relationships among the other realms, the intellect begins to analyze itself and its memories in cannibalistic catabolism, like a dragonfly eating its own tail.

In drama and in comedy, in cinema and on television, around the campfire and on the Internet, the audience agrees to suspend its disbelief of the realities of characters and situations, and accepts the play, the story, the ritual as utterly real and complete, a virtual reality accepted as actual. To participate in Mystery, the intellect must be expanded, to be more supple and relaxed than it usually is, to suspend its own disbelief. The intellect needs to be educated in the arts of perceiving symbols and metaphors, of interpreting them accurately and usefully, and of transmitting data in its proper categories to all the other realms/levels/tools/viewpoints.

Sometimes the intellect tries to censor the data it processes, usually when it's operating under identification with the individual self. This identification magnifies the influence of the astral planes, the survival urges that live there, and the emotions the urges generate. At other times, intellectual censorship occurs when data contradicts doctrine and dogma, seeming to attack faith itself. To progress in Mystery, it's necessary to maintain a sense of separation among the intellect, the thought it produces, that which perceives both, and the process of

thinking. This sense of separation is illusory, of course, but it can be useful in preventing intellect's identification with the information it processes.

When the intellect abandons its sword of analysis, and puts away its shield of skepticism, it becomes vulnerable to the dangers of propaganda, persuasion, disinformation and involuntary belief.

We have to be able to abandon a world-view when it no longer fits the data. We need to develop as many paradigms as necessary to communicate with other individuals in their own terms, without seeming to attack their premises, beliefs, or style. It's good to immerse yourself in strange paradigms wholeheartedly, with open intellectual acceptance during the visit. Intellect must learn to wait until all the relevant data have been acquired before analyzing, assessing and classifying the information, and then forming provisional conclusions about it. There are times when interim conclusions are needed to clarify decisions on procedure, perhaps the most common of which are "Is this present thread of inquiry worth its pursuit?" and "Where do I go from here?"

What does intellect have to do with Mystery? Isn't Mystery beyond intellectual analyses and conclusions?

Some might hold that Mystery, by definition, lies beyond the powers of intellect to comprehend it, that this inability of intellect to grasp a large truth is what constitutes the essence of Mystery. If intellect operated in isolation, this might be so; however, when linked with intuition, instinct, inspiration, integration and incarnation, it expands its capacity and grasp of information arriving from these sources. Intellect turns information into knowledge, and really enjoys doing it.

New information arrives constantly, and knowledge is

Chapter 13 :: Cosmic Visions

revised constantly. This seems to irritate people who desire Absolute Truth, people who resent change and who fear an uncertain future, people who really want the One True Way of salvation. Such attitudes are symptomatic of intellectual rigidity and/or paralysis. The operations of a rigid mind are often mechanically flawless; intellectual malfunction generally arises from false premises, from restricted topics of consideration, from use of learned logics and approaches (instead of discovered and inherent logics and approaches), and from filtered data. The flaccid intellect, on the other hand, can have free, accurate information and a variety of logics, yet it often errs through sloppy thinking. One common manifestation of a flaccid intellect is the mistaking of metaphor, and sometimes of simile, for direct description.

During my high school and college years, I used to dislike and object to the analysis of literature, particularly that of poetry and of plays. At the time, I felt that analysis somehow "killed" the subject, that in being forced to learn the underpinnings and basic structure of a poem or a play, I would no longer be able to immerse myself in the emotions and feelings it evoked. I was wrong. In learning the principles of literary engineering, I learned how to convey ideas as gracefully and as clearly as possible, as well as to appreciate the elegance of many writers. Analysis is necessary in the pursuit of Mystery and its truths as well as in art appreciation.

The search for Mystery has been going on for a long time among humans. Oral legends and myths, as well as fables with moral aphorisms, conveyed certain truths about the human condition, from the pragmatic and the practical to the truths encountered in the deepest of spirit journeys. All major Holy Books were written--and are being written--by mystics

Chapter 13 :: Cosmic Visions

and visionaries, and/or by their disciples, who try to convey their experiences to people who have not had the same level of experience. Commentaries are most often written by those devoted to the visions and words of a Mystic; Jesus didn't write the Gospels, Buddha didn't write the Sutras, and Mohammed didn't write the Quran. How far and how much can we trust these second-hand reports on the Masters' teachings?

How much has devotion and enthusiasm distorted inspired speech that's been set down in writing, how often have marginal glosses and scholarly notes been incorporated as part of the original words? It's impossible to determine exactly, but the intellect can compare your own experiences and insights with the various classical Holy Books of the major world religions. With training, your rational mind can distinguish among metaphors, similes and aphorisms, guarding your search for Mystery against the follies of literalism, of reading poetry as physical or spiritual fact, of mixing the planes of existence.

On the other hand, intellect can recognize patterns reflected throughout the observable universe, from the vast to the minuscule, patterns which are keys and clues to the nature of Mystery. It can find, among the multitude and complexity of things, resonances and commonalities that are echoes of Mystery. One of the best uses of intellect in the pursuit of Mystery is the monitoring of science news, in keeping current with discoveries about the physical world.

Intellect is also vital in monitoring, in interpreting and in discerning the influence of instinct on the quest for Mystery. With enough experience and training, the rational mind can distinguish between emotional responses to Mystery's radiance and emotional responses to physical needs, fears and desires.

Intuition resembles intellect in that it processes information

Chapter 13 :: Cosmic Visions

and reaches conclusions about it. Intuition differs from intellect in that it can skip steps required by logic, drawing on instinct and the Deep Mind to form useful opinions about a situation or idea. As intellect pares away the components of an idea or an experience in order to analyze the whole, intuition constructs an idea/experience and its expression through the gathering of images from personal memory, from myth and from its own interior vision, and fusing them into the complexity necessary for art.

Intuition's segment of imagination is sensual on many levels. It dresses ideas in the clothing of shapes, colors, sounds, scents, textures, flavors and auras of things. In the physical realm, the sensual imagination engages one's physical senses; in the astral worlds, the garb of idea appeals to the astral senses. The seeker of Mystery soon learns that astral images serve more to veil and conceal than to clarify and reveal. Outlines are blurred, the atmosphere is usually misty, and the layers of symbology are thick. Objects become clearer and firmer under your attention, but it's hard to hold an image for long; astral imagery is more fluid than that of the physical senses.

Intellect uses its part of imagination for numbers, flow-charts, structural diagrams, blueprints, geometry and other graphic presentations of information, for the most part. One new field in which intellect and intuition join forces is that of fractal geometry, where Byzantine-Paisley images build themselves from mathematical formulae through the iteration and recurrence of shapes. There's Mystery inherent in the operation of numbers, in constants derived from observation of nature, in complex shapes and patterns that are beautiful to see as well as to comprehend.

Intuition's work with imagination produces the fine and

practical arts to enrich our lives; it also produces the satisfying myths and legends that have guided behavior and provided explanations for Mystery throughout recorded and oral history. Intuitive imagery can also reveal or conceal the dark side of imagination. Consider the word presented differently: I, Mage; I, Nation. What does this suggest to you? To me, it says that imagination is the primary tool of the Magickian/Mystic, and that the experiences, discoveries, work, and essence of the Mage belongs to the species at large. The human nation shares the planet with many other nations (species). Perhaps our nationality extends to all sentience in the Cosmos. Why not?

The Mage shapes images for instructional purposes, but is subtle in technique. We do not preach, we use a light hand, we raise more questions than we answer. As artist, the Mage shows, rather than tells, weaving Mystery deep into the essence of the work, deeper than the relatively obvious language of symbols. At the same time, art in its many forms is a tool for exploring Mystery for the artist-Mage. We start with a central idea and its symbols, translating and transforming them into new imagery that reveals itself as it unfolds. In the process of intense creative activity, the sense of self disappears; the work seizes us in talons of rapture in which we see ever deeper into Mystery.

The term "imagery" here includes all the arts, graphic and otherwise. There are musical symbols to convey events through their emotional and mood components; the gestures, shapes and movements of dance express the same. And so on.

The Mystery of intuition will lead you to the dark regions of the soul, to the shadowy cosmos, to the haunted places. Although Western tradition stresses the need for a clear vision of your lighted, semi-enlightened self before descending into the worlds

Chapter 13 :: Cosmic Visions

of night, darkness haunts our dreams from childhood onward. Some of us shrink from it, while others approach it, fascinated. It's an honest piece of nature, not evil in itself, neither to be feared nor desired. Those who view the shadow romantically, goths, would-be vampires, Satanists, etc., are usually operating from uninformed imagination.

It's best to explore the fearsome dark whenever it presents itself to your attention, but wisely and strongly. It's part of Mystery that lives in the Deep Mind and in the vast gulfs between the galaxies. Intuitive imagination tends to clothe the forms of darkness as chimerae and monsters, especially in those whose imagination is influenced by fear of the strange, the alien, the unknown. When such forms are captured in works of art, they are well and truly bound until "higher" ways of exploration are available to examine them.

Draw your nightmares, play your fears, dance the darkness, sing with werewolf bards, sculpt the Old Ones. Ask your Deep Mind to reveal its mysteries of shadow. It's best to document each entity you meet in art, rather than let it drift about your consciousness unattended, perhaps to lay nasty eggs in the astral worlds.

How much of the art of darkness you should reveal to other people depends on your situation. There's usually no benefit in upsetting family, teachers or friends with presentations of their fears and with what they would consider evil, sick or insane. On the other hand, if you have a balance of "lightside" work to present with the darker ones, you may provide the beholder with enough paradox/incongruity to open his or her mind to transphysical realities.

Why do we find vampires to be sexy? What is there about the nature of incubi and succubi that draws us? Why have

Chapter 13 :: Cosmic Visions

there been so many religious proscriptions about sexuality? Beyond the straightforward reproductive drive of other animal species on our planet, humans have developed a complex tangle of emotional, psychological and spiritual factors around sex. Some of these factors deal with power over others by seduction and attraction, while others provide the pleasures of being seduced and attracted. There is also the factor of death in human sexual complexity; the inevitable end of physical life is echoed in "the little death" of orgasm, while the only means of "immortality" lies in the passing of our genetic information to a new generation through sex. The combination of these major chapters of human experience generate many tensions in our society. The tensions, in turn, produce some of the sense of darkness and its mysteries in the realm of intuition.

Intuition also deals with Nature: the kingdoms of mineral, vegetable and animal, the Cosmos at large, our fellow humans, and our own relationship to it all. Through intuition's sensibilities, we come to see our presence and functions within the Cosmos as a Mystery and as part of the larger Mystery of existence and being.

It was in the realm of intuition that I first noticed the similarities of various systems, large and small, that were encapsulated in the Hermetic aphorism "As above, so below; as below, so above." At the time, I called this general relationship of everything to everything else "the Universal Pattern of Consciousness" (see Chapter 2.) It's still sketchy in places, and seems to reveal itself to my mental peripheral vision rather than to submit to direct scrutiny.

The discovery of a universal pattern of consciousness led to other observations. Existence tends to complexity; simple things seem to find an advantage in joining with other simple

things to form an entity that contains them, an entity more intelligent and capable than any or all of its components. (The whole is greater than the sum of its parts.)

The best example available to the naked eye is the slime mold. Protozoa in forest floor leaf piles live placidly in moist conditions. When moisture becomes scarce, they congregate and link surfaces to become a sheet of tissue that crawls around, seeking damper ground. At a certain stage of maturity, the slime mold (the mobile sheet) extrudes towerlike structures that form spores on the tip. The spores, carried by the wind, drift down to the forest floor to become individual protozoa. Here, complexity confers mobility, vastly extending possible habitat for the protozoa and insuring their continuity.

When we exploded into existence as energy, our intelligence was latent in the power of our flight from our singularity of origin. When we slowed enough to acquire mass, charge, and spin, to be hydrogen, then gathered into stars and exploded again, our intelligence began to manifest in the variety of elements and their interactions. In the cradle of planetary gravity, the more complex molecules joined as cells, many of whom included such complex passengers as mitochondria. The intelligence of the cell resembles our own more than does the intelligence of molecules or that of pure energy. The cell has an interest in food, in metabolism, in avoiding harm, and in dividing into daughter cells. And so on up the line of complexity and organization, through hydras, sponges, starfish, squid, crabs, shark, fish, amphibians, reptiles, birds, marsupials, and mammals.

Human attainment of self-awareness as individuals has generated a fundamental error, that of assuming, as a species, that we're the crown of creation, and as individuals, that each

is the center of the universe. We're links in a chain, a band in a spectrum, well begun but obviously only half done—if that much.

We've not completed our journey to complexity. In my opinion, the search for Mystery leads to the next level, link, or band of manifested intelligence. The ecstasy that accompanies each minor unveiling of Mystery feeds our transformations as well as our perseverance. Learning about the universe we inhabit can generate a trance of wonder through our resonance with it. Even so, the glory of all existence is but another veil and gateway to further Mystery.

Chapter 14

Veils of Glory

When we consider our place in the cosmic scheme of things, one of the first things we notice is that we seem to be unique among earth's species. We have a type of self-awareness different from that of other animals, we've built technology-based civilizations, we have spoken and written languages, and we seem capable of behaviors so stupid that no other animal would manifest them.

In our dim and distant past, we convinced ourselves of the notion that, because we're more complicated and complex, we are somehow superior to the other animals. The author/compiler of the Book of Genesis describes the creation of Adam as the culmination of God's works. Galileo suffered house arrest by Church authorities for daring to support Copernicus' observation that the earth orbits the sun; the thought that the heavens didn't revolve around us was abhorrent enough to be heresy.

You, O lover of Mystery, know better than that—yes? In your spirit journeys, you've seen the magnificence of our universe. (I suggest you obtain access to the various photographs from the Hubble Space Telescope, and from the various exploratory missions to the outer planets of our system.) You've experienced the memories of your subatomic particles, atoms and molecules banged into existence and cooked in supernovae. You remember,

Chapter 14 :: Veils of Glory

however dimly, what it means to be a single cell, complex with proteins, sugars, mitochondria, and cilia. In the tropisms and experiments of time, you hold the history and the fact of increasing complexities and connections within the very structures of your body.

You have the experiences within you of huge changes of size and scale; from the infinitesimal to the vast at the beginning, living as stars and as the substance of stars, then becoming subatomic as we explode between gravity and atomic fire into clouds of dust and gas. We're now midway in complexity between the subatomic and the supergalactic, in body, mind and soul. We have our place at the heart of things.

Less well-known than the mistake of seeing oneself or one's family, clan, nation, or species as the crown of Creation is an attitude of unworthiness, of guilt, of shame for the sins of our fathers, as it were. While it's true that we've polluted the planet, destroyed other species, devastated forests and jungles, and committed genocide amongst ourselves, these have been the mistakes of a child, a clumsy adolescent. We're finally beginning to see the natural consequences of wrong action, and are attempting to remedy them.

It's from visions of ourselves as a mature and wise lot, visions of a future, that legends of a fall from grace arose. This doesn't mean that evil doesn't exist; it means that humans are not evil by nature. Much of the Western world is still waiting for a Savior to come, for the first or the second time, depending on your religion, to restore us to a state of perfection that never was.

Some people attempt to create an alternative reality in which to live, a reality in which we find what we seem to lack in the world of the outer senses. Some people do this in role-

playing games, either on a table or in houses and in woods. Some people join historical re-enactment groups, or organizations which meet to re-create the crafts, arts, and societies of the Middle Ages. Still others live in a world created by a favorite author, where they see themselves as "Free Amazons", as prey for Cthulhu, as secret agents, or as heroines of a romance novel. Problems arise when you neglect to ground yourself physically first, to have means of self-support and shelter for your temple. Living a secret life can help keep you sane if you can integrate it with the necessities of living in our current society. If you fancy yourself as a king, a goddess, a knight, or a sage, it's wise to refrain from remaining "in character" with family members, employers, or other authority types.

This third stance rises from experience at the beginning, from remembering the countless other universes exploding into being as we/ours did. These other universes reflect variants of events occurring in the first instants of existence. They coexist with our familiar cosmos as various AM and FM radio stations' broadcasts fill the air around us; our consciousness can tune in information on frequencies other than the one on which "our" universe plays. Part of Mystery is learning about these other universes, experiencing a sample of possibilities, extreme and subtle. One aspect of Magick/Mystery is that of locating and using the occasional gateways that link the probability-worlds. Time plays at different rates in many of the alternate worlds, and the forms developed by self-aware intelligence vary widely.

A form of a fantasy life is to regard oneself as non-human, as an alien in a human body, sent to observe human ways, perhaps, or to judge the species on its fitness to continue existing. This is an attempt to distance oneself from the "human condition", to deny that one is as much a naked ape as everyone else. It's taken

Chapter 14 :: Veils of Glory

me effort to accept my own membership in our species; only my own sins against intelligence and compassion could convince me to do so.

Let's assume that we have a realistic grasp of life in the middle of things, an appreciation of our physicality, our emotions, our mind, our creativity. We see how we fit in with the rest of the universe, but we still wonder about the why of it, the point, the meaning, even the responsibilities, of existence. Why do many of us need a communicative God (or Goddess)? Why do many of us fear death? Mystery surrounds the gift or curse of self-awareness, and so the nature of the self provides good hunting for the Mystic, as well as providing a major trap of infinite regression in self-reference. Tread lightly, and beware!

The sense of self is a major component of the Mystery we love and seek. Why do we know that we know, that we respond to both the knowledge and the knowing? What distinguishes you from other people, that anchors itself in your mind's flesh, that answers to your name? What does it take to make you happy, to satisfy you? What function in the grand scheme of things do you fulfill?

When you survey the history of the universe, you're seeing the history of your physical body as well as the patterns of complexity and simplicity that comprise your mind. When you review your personal Big Bang that began at the fusion of your mother's egg and your father's sperm, you can trace the complexity of your cells' multiplication and differentiation from the singularity of your zygote. When you recall your earliest childhood memories, you can see the impulses and experiences that have shaped your personality and philosophy into what they are today.

Even though we can trace our physical origins from the Big

Chapter 14 :: Veils of Glory

Bang, there still remain the Mysteries of mind, of intelligence, of soul. Does our brain generate mind as a field that persists for a lifetime, and perhaps beyond? Does our neural complexity simply provide a favorable environment for a universal consciousness to inhabit and use? Is there a God(dess) that crafts a soul and a consciousness for each individual at the moment of conception? If so, do twins share a soul, or is there a set of two waiting for their coming into being? What of triplets, or more? What is the "I" that is responsible for its own decisions and actions?

In the classic Eastern self-hunt of *neti-neti*, you begin by discarding from your consideration any component that is obviously not yourself. Is your body yourself? When you consider the phenomena of blood transfusions and organ transplants, the answer seems to be "no". The sense of self seems to be singular, losing nothing with blood and kidney donations, and gaining nothing with heart or liver transplants. If not the whole body, then what of the brain? I seem to live two inches behind my eyes and 3 inches or so from the top of my skull, but I don't seem to be attached to a structure. I seem to be the movement and patterns of the electric flashes among the cells, rather than the cells themselves.

Are your memories, your quirks and characteristics yourself? Not likely, since you can say they are your possessions. The same applies to your actions, moods, instincts, tendencies, thoughts, relationships, conditions, habits and experiences. All these things pertain to you, are possessed by you, even describe you, but, since you possess them, are not you. What a delightful, maddening Mystery! When all your possessions and characteristics are discarded, the center of their constellation appears to be empty. If so, what is it that experiences, decides,

Chapter 14 :: Veils of Glory

quests and questions?

Who speaks and who listens to the inner counsel that advises about the best course of action, or non-action? What suggests and what recognizes that there may, indeed, be entities who are more intelligent and more advanced than we are? What posits a "higher power" and names it "God"? Can the searching eye see itself?

Approaching the mystery of selfhood has two phases: the active discarding of all possessions, material, non-material and abstract, and the still, silent awareness of the nothing or something that remains. When you've reached the state of silent awareness, there's nothing to do except wait without striving. Since each individual experiences Inner truths in unique ways, I can't predict what will come to you in that silence, or whether you'll recognize it for what it is.

In my own experiences with visionary trance (or entranced vision), the *fact* shown, spoken, or otherwise inserted in my awareness was stunning. At the instant of comprehension I was unable to move, frozen in place and often breathless. The ability to move physically returned before the ability to think or respond emotionally. In some fashion, the visionary trance bypassed any instinctual reactions of fear or flight and overwhelmed me with the power and clarity of its content. The first feeling that returns, for me, is a sense of limitless exaltation, a destruction and subtler rebirth of the seeker and seer, followed by an awe and wonder that I can feel sinking in and spreading through all the layers of my being.

Rapture is a sense of being seized and swiftly carried upward, like a fish or a rabbit in the talons of an eagle or a hawk. Solid footing is gone, and struggle might result in a fatal plunge. There is often a sensation of being surrounded by and merged

Chapter 14 :: Veils of Glory

with light. In my own experience I've encountered a warm golden haze, a brightness of pure light, a silver-blue radiance as well as occasions of vivid, living darkness, a light beyond sight. In each case, the radiance is inhabited by an intelligence which stays at the edge of awareness, scarcely glanced, almost seen, haunting, familiar, and strange. The light and darkness pierce and penetrate every part of you, charging your vibratory rates with new energy while bearing its information into you.

I've never encountered a more immediate, intimate, intense, and all-inclusive experience than the realization of a hidden/obvious truth. Presentations to your Inner senses are more convincing than the physical world around you; most of us believe that there's a small chance of our physical senses malfunctioning, while we assume that our non-material perceptions are infallible.

Rapture invites total surrender. This is its function. By overwhelming instinct and experience, rapture peels you open to expose levels of yourself that conscious mind is barely aware of, if at all. It shows you a "you" tender, virginal, and impressionable. In surrender lies ecstasy. With surrender, you dissolve into the light and scatter on tides of bliss. No physical pleasure can even approximate that of realization's ecstasy.

Ecstasy can produce "miracles" of instant cures, stigmata, levitation, bilocation and apportation, often outside the awareness of the ecstatic, yet witnessed by observers. Suffusion with the visionary light sometimes produces glowing countenances and bodies, and the image of a halo is an artistic convention that echoes the strength of an ecstatic's visible aura. Ecstasy can also produce a perfume known as "the odor of sanctity." Many saints in the Canon of the Roman Catholic Church are ecstatics, safely dead.

Chapter 14 :: Veils of Glory

The image of Heaven that I formed during years of Catholic school was that of eternal ecstasy, ever dissolving in bliss, uniting with God in the Beatific Vision. The cartoon symbolisms of harps and halos are still taken literally by some Bible-believers, who seem absolutely unacquainted with metaphor. The idea of melting into the source of all being, forever, was so desirable that I despaired of ever attaining it, miserable sinner that I was (and perhaps still am.)

The problem with a Heavenly reward of union with the Godhead in limitless, eternal ecstasy is that the trail of Mystery leads beyond Heavens, ecstasies, visions, trances and realizations...and beyond Godhead as well. The light, the exaltation, the awe and wonder are veils that fill the Inner vision so well that the trailing cloak of Mystery is lost to sight.

We have our armor and censors to ensure our survival, to act as filters of the constant flood of information that surrounds us. Our physical senses are limited to a modest portion of the electromagnetic spectrum, to a certain range of sound, to the small amount of odors we can detect with our noses so far above the ground. We pay attention to only a small percentage of available data so that we can form essential judgements about actions that may save us or kill us.

We have defenses for our inner survival too, in a way, if by "survival" we mean our continuity with the views we learned and absorbed from early childhood, views concerning ourselves and the world we live in. It seems a part of human nature to learn quickly as a child, and then, as we mature, to settle on a philosophy or world view that gives us comfort and a sense of stability. Mystery disturbs comfort and stability; we like to feel that we have all the answers we need in order to get through life.

Chapter 14 :: Veils of Glory

Fortunately for the health and growth of our species, there are those of us who never lose the childlike qualities of curiosity, wonder and delight. These become scientists, artists, mages and mystics. The rigorous procedures of the scientific method, the observation, hypothesis, experiments, recording, theory, publication, then vindication or disproval, convinces us to accept the findings of scientists as true, useful, and as a rational increase of our collection of known things. The truth of the artists convince us by precise mixtures of the familiar and the strange that win us through resonance and memory.

The truths of ecstatic visions aren't gradual or rational; to the person who has achieved a working peace with the universe, the realizations of Mystery can seem violent, shocking and disruptive. The pleasure and bliss of rapture seems to be a life-support system for identity, for sanity, for continued incarnation. In a sense, rapture imposes a mode of consciousness that is at least an order of magnitude larger than our present one, whichever that may be, and the ecstasy keeps us alive long enough to grow to acceptance.

There seem to be various kind of visions, and the degree of rapture, if it's present at all, seems to match the nature of the information. Visions of the spacetime continuum, in its vastness and glory, can seize you on and through the physical plane as well as on and through the emotions, mind and imagination. When I was a child, standing under a clear night sky, I could feel the presence, as thick as touch, of countless intelligences beating above me. Great waves of longing passed through me, and I'd send out mental calls to my "star-brothers". As an adult, I've fallen up into the stars from a campsite sleeping-bag, and from gazing at the Milky Way in a dark country field.

Realizations on the astral planes are more dreamlike, more

lunar in nature, more fragmentary and more nebulous than are those of other faculties. It's possible to dissolve in moonlight, but I usually find myself floating in it or on it, rather than being absorbed by it. The kinds of truths seen and felt astrally are very old, older than the human mind. Visions here, in my experience, are more diffuse, but profoundly stirring, events.

Astral rapture, although often dreamy and symbolic, can also focus on strong, and often irrational, emotions. These can be evoked by an image, a symbol, a pattern of half-seen shadows, or they can even occur spontaneously. They can arise during a vision trance, or catch you by surprise as you go about your daily activities. Sometimes beginning Mages/Mystics feel that they're under attack from an unknown, invisible source; others feel spellbound to another person, known or unknown, feel a sudden love for our planet, feel great nostalgia for places they've never been, and so on. Depending on your stability and balance at the time, it's a good idea either to ward and protect yourself until you're in a position to explore these feelings, or to follow them to their deep origins. It's not a good idea to try to ignore or forget them. (See "Banishment" in Chapter 6.)

Realizations concern images, symbols, and meanings. Many visions in the astral realms concern Mystery itself, often personified and flowing through silver mist. The ecstasies of the moon are the beginning, for many who experience them, of Mystery's spellbinding sorcery. The ecstasy is that of enchantment or obsession, haunting you with longing for a touch of Mystery, leading you ever onward.

Vision trance of the intellect involves revelations of order, elegance, precision. My first experience in this was as a child, discovering the delightful fact that the integers in multiples of nine would also add up to nine. Later, the music of Bach would

Chapter 14 :: Veils of Glory

suspend me in wonder through its seeming inevitability of movement and counterpoint, crystalline and perfect. Pythagoras was another mentor of mind, not only with the Mystery of the golden rectangle, but also with the octaves of sound in a vibrating string.

There are clues of Mystery in the findings of every scientific discipline; if you combine the Hermetic dictum "As above, so below; as below, so above" with reports from the frontiers of science, the intellect's pattern recognition can transport you to breath-stopping heights. The rapture of the intellect wraps you in the splendor of all that is, chaotic and orderly, astonishing and familiar, holographic and unique. Straight lines are rare in nature, save for the planes and edges of crystals; all else is curved, simply and compound: stars, bubbles, planets, eggs, rainbows, impact craters, arteries, snail shells, DNA molecules, bones, liquid turbulence, and so on.

The intellect wants to entify Mystery, to assign it qualities; from the clues in the physical world, it hypothesizes that there's something curved about Mystery, something fluid and dynamic. It also notes that there are factors of edges and planes in the formula, something orderly and stable. Is there dualism in Mystery, or only in our perception of its shadow?

The vision trances of intuition have in them something from the other realms. From the physical plane come the shapes and movements of the natural world, the astral plane provides the raw emotions to be spun into finer, subtler versions, and the intellect lends a sense of pattern and order. The intuitive rapture arises as the blend of these influences reveal the universal pattern of consciousness in all things. The ecstasy confirms the self's relationship with all of existence, proclaiming you a child of the universe, and at the same time,

Chapter 14 :: Veils of Glory

an insignificant and mortal unit of life.

The gods were born in the rapture of intuition, as was our devotion to them. I've mentioned that in a way, religion arises from our need of safety and comfort, consolation and certainties. We create God not so much in our image and likeness as in the image and likeness of our parents. In the major Western religions, God is as stern, capricious, jealous, and vengeful as any human father. I suspect that a Mystic had influence in shaping the Christian religion, however, since the figure of Christ answers the need of lovable God, a brother rather than a father. Perhaps the real secret of Christ is that He incarnated so He could have a mother.

When you pursue Mystery into the heart of intuition, the rapture of its vision of the universe distills from awe and wonder a love too large for familiar human dimensions. Experience with our shortcomings encourages us to create and entify someone large enough, in every sense of the word, to receive and contain this love, to be this love, and to return it to us as desire for union.

It's wise to invest this love in Mystery itself, that it may draw you ever onward in your search.

Chapter 15

Self

Mystery has led you on a merry chase through the glories of the universe and of the planet you live on and in. The education and changes in perspective you've gained in the process generate more questions, but questions that are wiser and closer to the essence of Mystery. Inevitably, the trail loops, twists, dances, and leads right into yourself. Who and what is this self? Mystery here is so all-pervasive, omnipresent, intimate, and elusive that it can make your teeth itch.

A Vignette

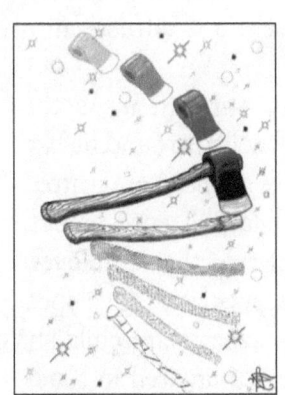

"Hey, George, that's a fine-lookin' axe you have there."

"Yep, been in the family for years. Used to belong to my great-great grandpa."

"Sure is in good shape for bein' that old."

"Ought to be. It's had three new heads and five new handles since we've had it."

Chapter 15 :: Self

I've heard that the cells in the human body are totally replaced every seven years, yet the body retains its integrity and identity. Are you the same person you were at age seven, or at fourteen? Has anyone ever told you "You don't seem to be yourself today," or "That comment was sure out of character"? When you look at photographs of yourself as a child, or read old diaries or poetry that you wrote years ago, do you marvel at how much you've changed? When you consider your desires and aspirations for the future, do you see the changes necessary in the development of your skills and knowledge that these aspirations demand? What is it that provides coherence and continuity between zygote and corpse, and that seemingly extends farther in both directions?

Memory seems to forge a thread common to all the selves we've been and are, vanishing into the mists of time at both ends. If we follow the thread, however, we see that it's not a single line of events concerning only ourselves, but more like a rope, net, or tapestry. Each of our ancestors gave half of themselves to our making, half of which is used in each generation, half of which spins off into "worlds of 'If'," the might-have-beens that never manifested in our version of reality. If we have descendants, the configuration is similar, as our genetic selfhood diffuses into our species at large.

Perpendicular to the flow of history through us is the constellation of aspects of our current self, belled around us like a dervish's coat. Some of these aspects we've deliberately crafted to smooth our way in life: the dutiful child, diligent student, efficient soldier, considerate lover, trustworthy employee, faithful spouse, informed citizen—all the aspects we've developed in relationship with other entities. Other aspects are childish, childlike, feral, and dark. These can emerge uninvited in times

Chapter 15 :: Self

of stress or with a strong emotion, delighting or appalling us and those around us.

One common factor of the aspects is that when one is manifesting, you are that aspect, sometimes automatically, sometimes deliberately, and sometimes under protest. Your ability to surprise yourself, to embarrass yourself, to impress yourself with an outstanding feat demonstrates that you are not monolithic, solid, or homogenized. Our subselves are not shards of a former integrated self; rather, they are stages of growth and experience accumulated and saved in memory, sometimes too deeply for our present consciousness to access easily.

As usual, words fall short in their power to accurately describe experiences beyond intellect's realm. There are similarities of consciousness to other models, such as holography, strange attractors, electromagnetic spectra, and so on.

Holograms are photographs made using a split laser beam; the resulting image presents a three-dimensional quality to the viewer. Looking at a hologram from different angles allows you to see its right side, left side, top, bottom and the usual frontal view. If a hologram is cut into pieces, each one contains the whole image, although at a fuzzier resolution than the original had. In such wise, consciousness varies in its qualities of clarity, detail, and capacity according to the complexity of the organism, or subself, supporting it.

The consciousness of an embryo just forming its neural tube is different from the consciousness of an adult with a functional brain; the consciousness of a human adult is different from the consciousness of our entire planet. The tropisms of an amoeba are qualities of consciousness, as are the nest-building instincts of birds, the tendencies of atoms to link together into molecules,

Chapter 15 :: Self

the reasoning of philosophers, and the ecstasies of Mystics. If we become familiar enough with our own consciousness, we can recognize its pattern on every perceptible scale in the universe. Simple or complex, all things share the universal pattern of consciousness. Realizing the commonality of consciousness in the course of seeking our own generates a rapture that seems to dissolve individuality into the whole, temporarily.

A strange attractor is an artifact of Chaos Theory that consists of lines or tracks representing all possible behaviors of a dynamic system. On paper, it looks like a tube made of snarled string. In three dimensions, I see it as the woven straw tube that traps inserted fingers, sometimes known as "Chinese handcuffs." In a sense, we are all of our possible behavior, not all of which are predictable by our present state of consciousness. We're not only our own history, but also our capacities and capabilities. There's an old U.S. Army recruiting slogan, "Be all that you can be," which, when used as a formula in our search for our essential self, can produce an ecstatic vision of what's been called Knowledge and Conversation of the Holy Guardian Angel.

I dislike the term "Higher Self" because it's simplistic and inaccurate. The self in search of itself, our "present consciousness," as it were, can be seen as a constellation of aspects collapsed around and in our physical body and our name. When we catch a glimpse of our extended self and see all of our aspects, especially those of the future and those of the alternative realities that surround us, we often interpret it as a superior Other; if not as a god or God, at least as an angel, as a power spirit, or as an alien somehow more advanced than we are. In the beginning of our inquiry into the essence of our self, it's accurate enough to regard such glimpses as contacts

Chapter 15 :: Self

with the mysterious Other since we're operating in the realm of duality.

If we use the electromagnetic spectrum model of self, our familiar consciousness would be the range of visible light, from the edges of the infrared to the boundary of ultraviolet. The spectrum below red is characterized by longer wavelengths and less energy; above violet, wavelengths are shorter and the energy is higher. The small segment that our eyes can see is in the midrange, like our physical size that falls midway between the realm of the subatomic and the super-galactic. Much of the nature of our self is invisible to normal human consciousness, which is why mystery-hunters have developed ways of altering ordinary consciousness in order to see beyond its usual limitations.

However apt a metaphor, it can only be approximate and partial. This is the danger inherent in Holy Books and mystical writings; the high tongue of poetry, poor limping vehicle that it is, can at best provide only sidelong glances at what it describes. When readers or listeners of descriptions of spiritual, Mystical, or Magickal truths take hints as objective reporting, and then form prescriptions and proscriptions of behavior, only mischief can follow. I recommend that you translate your visions and raptures into deeds rather than words, even though such a course makes you a mystery to others.

If you use the neti-neti process in pursuit of your essential self, you'll get the same results as when you used it on your physical, emotional, intellectual, and imaginative aspects. The constellation of subselves–past, future, and collateral–proves to be a collection of possessions orbiting emptiness. This emptiness, this void, this nothing still perceives, still feels real to itself, as though it were a sentient center of gravity for it possessions.

Chapter 15 :: Self

This emptiness, this hollow core, is the essential individual self, and yet it has location as the center, exhibits continuity through time, experience and change of state (waking, sleeping, dreamless sleep), and seems based upon, as well as anchored to, the physical body.

In a way, this formless awareness is generated by the development and evolution of the physical body, and by that body's experience and memory of the perceptible universe it inhabits. The dividing daughter cells of the original zygote are busy little animals, growing, cloning their genetic information molecules, and forming twins of themselves, clinging to each other, responding to their programming, and beginning to specialize, depending on their positions relative to each other. From the initial perfection of their collective form as a hollow sphere, the cells begin the labor of involuting, forming crude grooves and tubes destined to become spine and gut.

Growth in number and increasing complexities of forms and relationships among the cells generate an entity; cells become embryo, "they" become "it". This is the second perfection. The process of growth and specialization continues until the new individual can survive outside the womb, with senses ready to collect data and a neurosystem ready to process it. Even before the event of birth, the senses can perceive the sounds of its mother's heartbeat and muffled vibrations from the world outside, can sense movement and pressure, can distinguish light and darkness through its mother's distended belly.

When the increasing complexity of the individual reaches various thresholds of perception, the essential self is formed as the Observer. This is the third perfection. The process of birth suddenly floods all the senses with information; a radical mode of being begins as a contained, aquatic existence bursts

Chapter 15 :: Self

into freedom and air-breathing, noise-making, eating, and eliminating. New sensations of harsh light, shapes, hunger, satisfaction, varieties of touch, and the presence of very large Others rock the Observer with intensity and variety. When the Observer begins to distinguish between stimuli of pleasant and unpleasant kinds, and to notice, by means of the developing memory, patterns and repetitions of events inside and outside of the body, it attains a fourth stage of perfection.

As you grow through childhood, puberty, youth, and adulthood, experiences create your subselves through pleasure, pain, emulation, and reaction. At the time of its creation, each subself seems to be your essential self, and can remain in that seeming, until contradictory experiences convince the Observer otherwise. These experiential subselves often coexist with others in various phases of life; you can be a beloved child and nonvoting member of your family at home, an academic whiz in the classroom, a bully's victim on the playground, a leader-into-mischief among your friends, and a klutz on the baseball diamond, all at the same age. There are ties of relationship among your subselves as well as their primary links to your physical body and to your Observer.

Incidental mysteries accompany the Mystery of selfhood: do you survive physical death? Once the physical body is gone, does your spirit, your self, your primary Observer continue in existence without a vehicle to anchor it in the material universe? On the other hand, does your physical body "only" exist as a chrysalis in which your self grows until it's ready to hatch into a nonphysical existence? What does a discarnate person do to keep from being bored? Both the concept of eternal punishment and that of eternal reward strike me as horrid, even if they contain enough change and variety to

Chapter 15 :: Self

prevent apathy and stupefaction. Since change needs time in which to happen, and since eternity denotes an absence of time, the Western religious ideas of heaven and hell have to be static conditions.

The concept of the afterlife as a continuation of physical life seems to have been a popular belief in many cultures for millennia. Archeological investigations have fond grave goods (provisions for the afterlife) in the form of tools, jewelry, furniture, containers of food, clothes, chariots, and even rows of terra cotta warriors, in burial sites around the planet. The afterlife, be it Valhalla, Summerland, Paradise (with self-restoring houris), the Western Land, or Amenta, is pictured as a never-ending cycle of the joys of life in the flesh.

The idea of reincarnation has its merits; I've experienced what seem to be memories from past lives, none of which were verifiable by historical research, but plausible and familiar-feeling at the times I experienced them. (It's amusing how many true believers in reincarnation identify themselves with major figures of history, as though there were a Cosmic Copier that clones the selves of the rich and famous for wide distribution.)

From the glimpses I've caught of the nature of the Observer and its satellite subselves, I think our postmortem existence offers a mix of options. Those who proclaim a single fate for all, be it paradise/perdition, reincarnation, functioning as ancestors for the living family members who consult us and make offerings to us, dissolution and dispersal, life review/debriefing, and so on, are much like the blind men and the elephant. Just as judging the proverbial pachyderm by touch alone yields only the partial notions that it's like a wall, a tree, a rope, a snake, and so forth, so do visionaries take their own glimpses of the afterlife as inspired truths about "the way it is."

Chapter 15 :: Self

Bearing this in mind, explore the subject for yourself (pun intended). You don't need to put yourself into a trance state; just turn your attention to your Observer, your essential self, and ask it to share its full experience of existence thus far. "Aha!" you might exclaim. "If I'm talking to 'my' Observer, then it can't be my essential self, can it?" Mystery alert! Observant of you. Could it be that whoever questions the Observer isn't exactly you anymore?

If you're very quiet, and pay close attention to your Observer, you may well learn things you never suspected you know. You might be presented with past lives scenes, you may see a preview of this life's end, you might be gifted with silent knowledge about how it all works, or you may only feel the touch of the trailing veils of mystery. If you do realize something about the continuity of identity, before and/or after death, examine it in the light of traditional views on the subject to see how, or if, it fits in.

My own explorations have yielded some provisional findings about the self and the phenomenon of death. The manner of death seems to make a difference in the kind of experience waiting for the newly departed. In an expected, accepted death, you travel lightly, with very few issues to resolve. Although time operates differently on the astral planes, a version of it still exists. You spend about forty days in your astral body, making peace with your new condition, saying goodbye to loved ones and to favorite locations on the physical plane. When you feel ready to move on, you will your astral body to dissolve, consign it to the elements, or symbolically eat it.

The subselves generated from your basic instincts are attached to your astral body, by and large, and should be properly disposed of at this point, before you move into the

realm of ideas and intuitions, the so-called etheric plane. If you are in a culture that reveres the ancestors and you subscribe to the idea of their usefulness, you can anchor your astral body, its natural subselves, plus appropriate subselves of other levels, to that reverence by a permanent command of service. The anchorage is linked to time and its passage; after your name is forgotten, your donated portions will be subsumed by the general ancestral collective. You can use a similar process for a planned haunting, but chances are good that you've resolved petty motives in the process of accepting your death.

In an expected but unaccepted death, you have a harder time and spend more relative time in the astral body. You strive to understand the perceived injustice of your situation; sometimes you have to resolve strong feelings of revenge against a person or people who were a proximate or remote cause of your death. This most often happens in cases of legal executions, of death in battle, of a surgeon's insufficient skill, of an industry's toxic pollution. Sometimes the non-acceptance arises from strong emotions of love, from frustration about unfinished work, or from other kinds of positive attachment.

You may attempt, and even succeed at, haunting the source of your protest, until you realize that no amount of interplane contact will change the fact that you've died.

Unexpected death by accident or catastrophe can mean a period of confusion on the astral plane, depending on your general understanding of death and its stages while you lived. The shock of sudden passage can "freeze" your capacities of comprehension for a while, especially if you've been a devout materialist in life. Confusion can happen if you die in coma, in dreamless sleep, or while unconscious. Since the astral realms are shaped, to some extent, by our expectations and

Chapter 15 :: Self

assumptions, the world you awaken to can resemble physical reality at first. When the apparently solid environment begins to dissolve into the fluidity of its astral nature, it's easy to think you're hallucinating or going insane. If you die while dreaming, you're notified of the fact by the content of your dream.

It's wise to factor in considerations of your death in each stage of your Mystical/Magickal growth. In the traditional Abramelin Operation, you invoke your Holy Guardian Angel in a months-long retreat of prayer, concentration, ritual purity, and dedication. After union with the Angel, you evoke and bind demons, establishing command over them as servitors to your purpose. Translating this tradition as metaphor, you order your subselves into a balanced and harmonious configuration. Be sure to include among them subselves of a corpse, a skeleton, and a heap of dust.

Operating in the dimension of time, there's an apparent hierarchy of subselves from the simple and primitive to the complex and sophisticated, strung like beads on the intangible thread of self, which is knotted at intervals with other threads into a net. Our ordinary consciousness can perceive the subselves of the past and present once it learns how to see; the future "higher" subselves are hazy in different degrees of probability. Union with the Angel is an analog of opened perception of the self.

Outside of time, memory works in all directions. It's not limited to the past, since the past is part of time. It recalls the future, as it were, connecting the more complex, the more refined subselves that we *will* to be, aspects that make us glad to be ourselves, with simpler, naïve, erroneous, and sometimes twisted aspects. Outside of time, none of our subselves are denied by other aspects that "know better"; nothing dark about

Chapter 15 :: Self

us is rejected or deliberately forgotten. Instead of evoking our "demons" into constraining triangles after invoking our "angel" into a protective circle, we call all subselves to visibility in a sphere around us, beings of light and shadow ranged on their own points of latitude and longitude.

And the sphere begins to sing.

The older, darker aspects sound the bass notes and rhythms: low, profound, monk-chanting, thunder-rumbles. Half-lit aspects build midrange chords, resolving dissonances, modulating in and out of strange patterns. High, pure voices of future selves ring like stars, the whole in harmony as complex and shifting as the Northern Lights. The song of the self links and locks the aspects in exquisite vibration. Hues, sounds, textures, scents, and flavors coruscate over and around the sphere like the colors on a bubble, or ocean waves, or the play of wind in reeds.

The innate harmony of the self intoxicates with rapture, suspends thought, floods all feelings with glory and awe. Drunk with ecstasy, you dissolve and reform at the center of the sphere, expanding to fill and surround it, radiating through its interstices, realizing your beauty, secure in your balance, aware at a new level.

This new awareness rides your radiance, streaming outward in all directions, touching everything around you in joy and compassion. In the simplicity of your united complexities, you wonder at the sorrow you find, so many sleepers mired in nightmare, confusion, pain, and fear. You have awakened to your beauty; can they not awaken to theirs? As your subselves have fused to become the completion that you now are, could not these sleepers join with you to become an even greater entity, were they awake? Even as they sleep, are they not you, in a gray and minor union?

Chapter 15 :: Self

From compassion grows determination and unlearned knowledge, a will and a plan to awaken the sleepers, to embrace them, to see them rise to joy equal to your own. You burn with love for them, and for what you become with them. Unafraid of pure passion in your rapture, you vow integrity of self anchored in physical reality until all sleepers wake.

You wed yourself to the wheel of birth and death without constraint, save that of compassion, of molten love. (In a corner of your mind, the morning call of "Come on now, rise and shine!" takes on a new and stunning meaning.) You pledge no gentle, and possibly ineffective, hand to your task. You remember your own stubbornness and reluctance to change, to see, to admit the need for any transformation. How you clung to your nightmares, and how they cling to theirs!

As your flesh-body summons your return from rapture and vision trance, you know your life has changed profoundly. You mask your radiance in normalcy, and seek to study shadow, to learn the essences you'll need to tame the nightmare realm to your task. Light to light, dark to dark, you tune your song of self to the resonance of the sleepers.

The self-known are not necessarily "nice."

Chapter 16

Shadow Mirror

There is more than unity of the subselves in the rapture of harmony and beauty; you plumb the depths of yourself, and the depths that you consider to be beyond yourself. Could it be the realm of instincts and reaction that you need to search, shadowed by the past as it is, for the dimensions of evil and imbalance that none can deny in the realm of identity? The Mystery of evil is as old as philosophy. It's not enough to simply acknowledge that it exists; we must understand it intimately if we're to transform ourselves. Mystery leads us first to the shadow mirror of the self so we can see individual evil. Later we encounter evil (so called) in its subtler, cosmic guise.

Does evil exist outside of human thought and action? Are there fallen angels who inspire us to wrongdoing, or aliens bent on our destruction, enslavement, or corruption? Satan is a popular figure in Western Christendom, first seen in the Book of Job as the Adversary; later, he became an enemy of God in contention for human souls. (In my opinion, it takes a measure of spiritual pride to imagine that human souls are worth fighting over on such a cosmic scale. It takes even more audacity to blame the results of our own actions on one or the other contender.)

We use the metaphor of darkness to signify evil, but the dark earth of the sprouting seed and the dark uterus of the

Chapter 16 :: Shadow Mirror

developing fetus are rarely considered evil. We use the metaphor of light to represent good, but exposure to sunlight can cause skin cancer and cataracts. Many fear death and consider it to be a major evil, but is it? All that lives will eventually die; does our fear of an event make it evil? Much of our thought and action is based on unquestioned assumptions, and much of our assumption-based thinking and doing result in damage to ourselves and to others. Is complacent ignorance the true essence of evil?

Is the much-revered innocence of childhood proof against it?

When I was about six or seven years old, my neighbor and playmate, Mary Ann, and I would alternate being the characters in a game we called "The Baby and the Witch." The figure of the witch as an epitome of evil was derived from various traditional fairy tales and from animated films from the Disney studios. We weren't much concerned about the background of the situations or the origins of the baby or the witch, but each episode we played opened with the baby firmly in her clutches. The point of the game was to invent ever more ingenious tortures for the witch to perform on the baby, and then to act out the evil events with imaginary props in imagined settings.

There are only two specific tortures I can remember. The first consisted of putting ground glass in the baby's formula bottle, and the other was the witch presenting the baby with a beautiful rocking horse with all the legs sawed almost through. When the baby clambered on and began to rock, the legs would break and tumble the baby to the floor where it would break a few bones and perhaps sustain a concussion. I think the most perverse aspect of the game was the great glee and joy of power we found in being either character, in finding the same pleasure

Chapter 16 :: Shadow Mirror

both in the giving and in the receiving of imaginary pain.

My parents were kind and decent people, and to the best of my knowledge, so were the parents of Mary Ann. We'd invented the game on our own, just for the fun of pretending to deliberately cause pain. We were never caught, and eventually we grew bored with it. The memory of that game stays with me over the years as an icon of innate evil from and in the minds of children.

Are nonhumans capable of evil? What of the cat, toying with its prey before killing, and sometimes eating it? What of the wolverine, scourge of trappers, who seems to savage and rend any vulnerable animal it can find without necessarily eating it? Is there a level of intellectual sophistication that generates an innate dimension of morality in an entity's actions? Perhaps we anthropomorphize when we speak approvingly of a dog's loyalty and devotion and shudder at a sow's devouring her piglets.

On the other hand, what of intelligences of greater sophistication than our own, be they extraterrestrials, higher orders of being, or our descendants? Is evil particular to our present state of comprehension, or are more developed minds capable of an evil more profound than our own? Would the existence of such a capacity imply its employment? I think writers of horror novels and makers of horror movies have tapped into an intriguing fear in their depictions of strange beings whose powers are superior to ordinary humans', whose motivations are obscure, and whose actions cause panic, pain, and death. Our xenophobia translates into wealth for those who know how to manipulate it and into the evil of restriction for those who accept its visions as reality.

Almost everything we can say about evil has to be couched

Chapter 16 :: Shadow Mirror

in human terms, in tribal terms, or in personal terms.

The mystery of evil and good has been a major concern of organized religions for centuries. Good is God's exclusive property, and evil belongs to the devil. We give God the qualities of omniscience, omnipresence, infinite love, interest in human doings, jealousy, judgment, and the ability to eternally reward good humans and punish bad humans. To the devil, we assign the qualities of pride, arrogance, hatred of God and hatred of humans, the ability to successfully tempt humans into doing bad things that will anger God, and the presidency of the place of human and demonic punishment.

God has a gang of servants called angels; the devil has a gang of servants called demons. All of the above have an interest in the doings of humans. The stories of creation, sin, captivities, conquests, deliverances, and downfalls in the Bible, the book of God's Chosen People, and its addendum, the New Testament, are full of contradictions and of human characteristics projected on cosmic figures. One of the greatest mysteries of Western religion, or of any religion, for that matter, is its persistent popularity. It would seem reasonable to expect that in this age of scientific discoveries about the nature of the universe, more people would be able to see the hand of man in the creation of God and his required Adversary.

Other religions worship or honor nature spirits, ancestors, and pantheons of gods and goddesses who act like humans. Some consider the head of state to be divine, and others have, at the core, transcended the notion of deity, but are tolerant of the human need to have something to placate and petition. Both theism and atheism have backed political groups and reigning dynasties, uniting the governed populace through a particular belief system into an obedient power base for the leaders. Why

Chapter 16 :: Shadow Mirror

do ordinary people enthusiastically accept such situations? What need does religion, even atheism and scientism, fill?

One of Aleister Crowley's better bits of rhyme says:

> *We place no reliance*
> *on virgin or pigeon.*
> *Our method is science*
> *our aim is religion.*

The word "religion," re-*ligare*, means a reuniting or rebinding of humans to God, based on the notion that there once was an unbinding, a separation, a fall from grace, as it were. Why do we consider that we were ever "better" than we are now? Where did the idea arise that we somehow lost a perfection in the past? Why have we posited the existence of Eden, Atlantis, Lemuria, Mu, Vril, and Shangri-La?

I've heard it said that the spiritual fall of humanity, the allegorical eating of the fruit of the Tree of Knowledge of Good and Evil, represents our self-perceived difference from the rest of nature. There seems to be a consensus that only human beings are capable of doing evil; the destructive/deadly agents of nature are innocent of harmful intent, incapable of harmful intent.

What distinguishes humans from the rest of nature besides our capacity to do evil? Could it be the type, extent, and application of the knowledge we have, and our type of intelligence that permits us to have and use that knowledge?

In my own experience of pursuing this facet of Mystery, I've seen that evil arises from imbalances and conflicts in our programming, as it were. Our various survival instincts, both the personal and the species type, were acquired and retained

Chapter 16 :: Shadow Mirror

in layers, much as our brain structure has its more primitive features covered by more recent and more sophisticated ones. Our uneducated sense of self resides in the middle of the layers, prodded into, and restrained from action and thought of various moral flavors by instinctual influences.

In Chapter 2, I outlined the survival instincts, or Forgotten Ones, and mentioned the functions of each. In the shadows of evil we see the reflections of the Forgotten Ones striving for dominance and expression in situations of ethical and moral choices. Imbalances in a Forgotten One tend to produce extremes of the instinct involved, extremes of lack and surfeit, which often clash violently with our other instincts and their effects.

Hunger extends itself to things we need, or think we need, to survive as individuals. In excess, it produces greed, avarice, gluttony, miserliness, selfishness, hoarding, and similar evils. Inadequate responses to hunger include apathy, sloth, neglect of one's own health, and that of one's family and animals. Famine and death are specters of hunger, and on the astral planes, its shadows take form as devouring ones who are never satisfied–vampires, lamia, and parasites of the soul.

Hunger lends its force and basic simplicity to the more specialized instincts. It would be fair to say that no Forgotten One acts alone; what we explore here are the instincts according to their predominance in each situation. Thievery in various forms has its roots in hunger, for instance, but the fight-or-flight instinct keeps watch, and the intellect is used to plan the theft. There may be emotional and egoic factors, such as gloating over one's cleverness as a sign of superiority over others. There could be a touch, more or less deluded, of the Robin Hood ideal of robbing the rich to give to the poor, as a highly individualized

Chapter 16 :: Shadow Mirror

idea of justice. It's an interesting exercise to analyze the classical sins and vices in order to see the interplay and distortions of the survival urges that generated and comprise them.

The Forgotten One of sex has a seemingly endless repertoire of types and manifestations. Sex influences our individual actions, social relationships, employment, civil and religious opinions, and many other aspects of life. With too strong an instinct for sex, it's difficult to concentrate attention on other matters, to honor oaths and vows, to realistically assess a situation of danger or control, to act in enlightened self-interest. Lust is obsession, whether it's focused on another person or is more concerned with one's own relief and/or satisfaction. With a weak sexual drive, a person often becomes overly cerebral, or acquisitive, or engaged in control of the behavior and thinking of other people. Sometimes having a drive weaker than another person's allows you to control the lustful one by keeping him or her on the mindless edge of desire.

Specters of imbalanced sexuality, particularly in the early twenty-first century, are pestilence and death. We are faced with AIDS, various forms of hepatitis, chlamydia-induced cancer and other sexually transmitted diseases, some of which are fatal. On the astral planes, incubi and succubi (thought to be two manifestations of the same entity), lamia, werewolves, ghouls, and vampires gather to feed on sexual energy and that of its connected sources.

When sex and hunger aren't balanced and coordinated with each other, we find our species in a situation of overpopulation, which adds the specters of war and famine. When a population of an area grows too numerous for the resources of that area, the people migrate, or send forces to take the resources of other people. The Forgotten Ones of fight-or-flight and clanning are

Chapter 16 :: Shadow Mirror

also engaged in this process, participating as both cause and effect. In a sense, the combinations of imbalances among these instincts manifest the wisdom of nature, in that war helps trim our numbers, as do famine and pestilence, through death. Advances in technology, manufacture, trade, and travel have changed the causes, courses, and methods of war. The condition of war persists, however, and it remains until our species learns a larger thinking than we currently use. I say "a larger thinking," rather than "a larger way of thinking," since it must include new ways of thinking as well as a better knowledge of our universe and ourselves, a better understanding of available data, and a comprehension of the wisdom of enlightened self-interest.

Venus and Mars were lovers in the mythology of ancient Rome. Ishtar/Astarte is a goddess of love and war. Sex makes babies who grow up to be generals and cannon-fodder; irrational sex is a major source of evil. The instinct of sex is a power source difficult to capture, tame, and use creatively, but we see the results of not doing so in the misery of the world, and in much of our own personal misery. One of the major problems in disciplining sex to serve the aims of transformative intelligence is its sheer psychic size. Our juices betray us; we're awash with the chemical commands of our little god DNA, and the torrent deafens us to subtler voices.

When you search for the Mystery of the basic instincts of earthly life–hunger, fight-or-flight, and sex–the form of your visions depends on your current perception of the world. If you've had problems with these Forgotten Ones, if their interactions and manifestations have been turbulent and problematic in your life from within yourself, or from within your family and friends, you may well encounter monsters

and demons. If your rapture is one of real prey, a paralysis and suspension in horror and helplessness, lean into it.

Strengthened by the memory of the coordination of your subselves into a self-aware unity, embrace the visions of the extremes that sex, fight-or-flight, and hunger can create. If you've avoided facing them previously, it could be that you thought that if you entertained these visions in your astral environment by means of your imagination, you might act them out in the physical plane, as either victim or perpetrator. On the contrary: in a form of spiritual martial arts, as it were, you more than cooperate with the nature and direction of your dark subselves and the instincts that drive them. Instinct compels our behavior by means of emotion; by evoking a Forgotten One with the aim of understanding it from the inside, we are immersed in strong emotion. Strong emotions can become addictive.

Each individual has his or her own ways of astral and spiritual perception; take advantage of your own. Some of us are visually adept, and see animated shapes and forms, terrifying and seductive, when we look into darkness. Others hear monsters and their activities in snarls, howls, slithers, hisses, growls, maniacal laughter, moans, whistles, screams, and raspy breathing. Still others encounter physical responses to the presence of a dark subself in the form of a wash of sexual heat, hunger pangs, an adrenaline rush, vertigo, panic, and so on.

With practice, you can develop your perceptions to the point where you're using all your inner senses in balance.

No matter your methods of perception, the principal means of understanding and integrating a dark subself with the self you know is to outweigh, outmatch, and outclass it, while using its own force to do the work for you. You've already united

Chapter 16 :: Shadow Mirror

your subselves; it remains to your conscious mind to know and understand them all.

The first lesson for you and a subself to learn is that you tame instinctual force by satisfying it (in responsible ways), and, where needed, by helping it get a little too much of what it considers a good thing. The internal wiring of an integrated self engages body, mind, and spirit with our various subselves, so an image-creating/sound making/emotion-triggering event occurring on one level is perceived and responded to on the other levels as well. When you create a scenario in the astral theater, as it were, it's real for your instincts, provided you've included those elements that are important to them.

For example: you're on a foray in the shadows, and you find the root of a major problem in your life, the unrequited desire for an unattainable person. Your rational mind has been wrestling with your obsession, to no avail. You've found yourself daydreaming about him or her, spinning fantasies, neglecting other matters that you know need your attention, alienating yourself from other people. You're tired of the frustration and hopelessness of the situation, and you want to put an end to it. Here's your chance.

In your mind's eye, your imagination, picture the desired one returning your desire, with open arms, soulful eyes, radiating sexual heat. See the two of you embracing, kissing, delighting in each other's touch, making love, shattering in orgasm, luxuriating in the afterglow, becoming aroused again and repeating the process. Over and over again, run the action until it becomes boring. Begin noticing his or her imperfections, annoying habits, and character flaws, projecting their development with age. Envision growing old together, bound together by inertia and bitterness, lacking the energy to leave

Chapter 16 :: Shadow Mirror

each other, waiting for death, dull-eyed and slack-jawed.

Back in your normal consciousness, if the person comes to mind, call up your astral scenario in memory, run it on fast-forward, and hold the final image. After this happens a few times, the final image will superimpose itself on the face of the person, injecting an automatic indifference into desire and neutralizing the former obsession.

This process, with appropriate modifications, can be used on any demon you encounter among or in your dark, instinctual selves.

When I was in grade school, perhaps in the fourth or fifth grade, there was an obnoxious boy in my class named Johnny S. He was a bully to the smaller kids, and a shouter of taunts and nasty comments to the girls. Most of my unpleasant encounters with him were at the bus stop after school was over. I had no desire for a physical fight with him, but I didn't like the buildup of anger in me. I set up an astral scenario (with no idea of the terms for what I was doing), where a beneficent but anonymous Authority issued me a license to kill, applicable only to Johnny. My favorite variation was to weight my book bag with bricks and bludgeon him to death with it.

The visceral satisfaction the scenario provided each time I ran it began and powered a feedback loop. From the satisfaction came a calm and a relaxation of tension and stress. From the calm arose an understanding that Johnny was enjoying the control provided by verbal and physical dominance, and that the ideal place to sever this control was in my responses to his aggression. The understanding generated a mild pity that Johnny couldn't communicate in a more effective fashion, and a great relief in me. After the scenario refused to hold together, I lost interest in participating. Since reporting Johnny's bullying

Chapter 16 :: Shadow Mirror

of the younger kids to the school principal was the only option I saw at the time to curb his behavior, an option I'd exercised at the beginning of the situation, I began waiting for the bus at the next stop along the route to avoid him.

Moral commandments that we find in religions and the legal codes of government serve a useful purpose for our species, inasmuch as fear of punishment and hope for reward keep many people from harming themselves and others. Moral and legal codes have helped us to survive thus far, as they seem to be necessary to keep the results of ignorance within acceptable limits. The moral territory claimed by religious commandments is larger than that claimed by law or custom, in that it goes beyond sins of word and deed by including sins of thought. The concept of "entertaining sinful thoughts" holds that thoughts or ideas are as significant as speech and action, not only for their ability to instigate action, but also for the pleasure they often provide to the thinker.

Before we've integrated our subselves in a balanced identity, it can be dangerous to fantasize scenarios of lust, revenge, and other instinctual impulses; when one is ignorant of astral possibilities, it's natural to act on the physical plane. This is a reason not to pursue the mystery of evil before we're established in our identity and balance. Another reason is that if we enter the shadows of our dark side before we understand that everything we meet here is our own, is us, we might well conclude that we're beset by devils, surrounded by demons, or victims of magickal attacks.

Why pursue acquaintance with our wild and scary parts after identity integration? To understand them and include them in the integration, and to learn the nature of shadow and darkness. This is not the last encounter with the imbalance

Chapter 16 :: Shadow Mirror

of evil; it's wise to pay attention, in detail, to the sources of mindless reaction now–you'll be meeting them again.

Mystery's trail winds through wide and wild terrain.

Chapter 17

That

It's true that nothing truthful can be said about "That," which is beyond language to describe. Who speaks? Who listens? The effect of That upon matter and consciousness can be felt, or otherwise sensed; words can point to and hint of these effects. The high tongue of poetry is best suited to expressing the manifestations of Divine Intelligence, the art of metaphor and sound, but even simple verse has its uses.

> *As I was walking up the stair*
> *I met a man who wasn't there.*
> *He wasn't there again today–*
> *Oh, how I wish he'd go away.*
>
> – H. Mearns

There comes a point in the pursuit of Mystery when rapture no longer accompanies profound spiritual realizations. It saves itself for simple beauties and small poignancies. What seems to occur in its place, at each new unveiling of mystery, is a quiet "Ah!" of delight as you dissolve into the further expansions of viewpoint such unveilings inspire.

The quieting and nonappearance of rapture is not a sign of jaded sensibilities, but rather a recognition that ecstasy is

Chapter 17 :: That

yet another illusion. Illusion, which is everything describable, tangible, and extant, is not to be regarded as inferior to the ineffable That, since illusion is included in That. (In the most tenuous of ways, That is also included in illusion.) Illusion, in all its kingdom, power, and glory, is art material, the stuff that dreams are made of.

What is the point, or the value, of making a distinction between illusion and reality? It's an Eastern stance that many Western mystics and philosophers agree with and find useful. It keeps Mystery beyond the reach of the seeker while work and experience hone and refine him or her for the revelations to come. We need dualism to navigate the open passages of Mystery to provide contrast, consonance, drama, and decisions in art, and to make the currents of manifestation flow. In itself, however, dualism is too narrow a view or a tool; perhaps it would be more accurate to speak of multiplism as more accurately reflecting our experiences in a multiple-choice world.

Early in Mystery, we learn the *neti-neti* process in our search for our essential self. We've identified all our possessions as not-I, and we found that the center is hollow. If you repeat the *neti-neti* now, you may notice that the central hollow has a complex shape, that it's not a smooth sphere. The irregularities of our individual voids constitute personality, enabling us to know (or tricking us into believing in) ourselves and others as separate people.

When we expand our conscious sense of identity to include the entire cosmos, on the other hand, we find that it, too, is complex and irregular, if not downright lumpy. Mind would like it, as well as our hollow core, to be regular and smooth, to achieve mathematical and topological perfection. Not since we were a singularity at the beginning of the Big Bang did we even

Chapter 17 :: That

resemble simplicity.

If there is enough dark matter in the cosmos, we'll have a Big Crunch when all the emanations of singularity converge. I see the universal explosion/expansion and implosion/shrinkage as a cycle in a pattern of cycles, like breathing or heartbeats. It's not a mechanical repetition, however; accumulating experience produces subtle changes in each cycle.

Since spacetime is an attribute of the material world and its harmonics (astral, etheric, mental, and other levels), all the cosmic explosions and implosions exist at once, like the petals of a chrysanthemum or the tendrils of a sea anemone, in the void. This world of worlds (the countless awakenings and sleeps of Brahma, as it were) is Maya–seemingly solid, but composed of one extremely busy thing stretched among nodes of nothingness.

Simple dualism is a crude tool. How far can we push dichotomy before it falls apart in our limited minds? What dualism can exist beyond that of plenum and void? Is there a difference between reality and illusion?

As our Eastern colleagues have declared, "Thou art That, I am That, all this is That." Why do we need the pronouns, then, of "thou," "I," and "this?" The first response is: because it's fun, it's the creation of art and beauty. Further consideration yields more sober reflections in the funhouse mirror.

Our minds love dualism for its providing contrasts and extremes. Black and white are easier to work with than shades of gray. We tend to imagine that the neurons of our brains, which respond to and generate some of the processes of thought, either fire or they don't, on or off, ones or zeros, in a basic binary code. Plenum and void are easier to comprehend as a pair of opposites rather than as a unit or as a sheaf of

Chapter 17 :: That

gradations.

Life requires differences and opposites, as do science, art, thought, love, perception, desire, and religion.

Where there is no difference, there is no tension, no gradient, no flow of energy, no work possible. Without opposites, charges aren't built, DNA isn't mixed, middle ways are obscure. Only within the sphere of illusion does time pass, do species evolve, do stars arise and die. In eternity, nothing changes.

Must our little selves choose between opposites? Are we restricted to black or white when we know not only shades of gray, but a whole spectrum of colors? When our focus is on physical reality, getting and spending, perhaps laying waste our powers, must we forget chaos and cosmos united in That?

Our flesh bodies anchor us to the spacetime continuum through the demands of thirst, hunger, fatigue, and discomfort. We don't have to forget our visions while we do our necessary work in the physical world, however. We can be mindful of our experiences in Mystery without being distracted by them; they become a background awareness in the rounds of daily life. The background can switch to foreground when you direct your attention to it.

Flesh life still presents situations of stress, danger, boredom, grief, desire, and other conditions, even after you've transcended them in your visions. The difference now is that, by reviewing your journey, you see problems and pain in context of the cosmos at large as well as in the immediacy of your life. This doesn't necessarily diminish pain in the level of existence you feel it, but it reinforces the fact that pain is temporary and that it occurs in a larger context. Pleasure is That and pain is That.

Is That Mystery? So it would appear. Nothing true can be said of it; it can be experienced, but not described. While

Chapter 17 :: That

we're still in the flesh, we can expect only glimpses of That, at best. More often, we mistake the light for its source, netting ourselves in the glory surrounding That.

Touching/awakening to That often breeds insights and speculations on death and eternity. Beyond our spacetime continuum, That thoroughly permeates it and imagines it in existence. Our individuality and identity depend on space and time; we change through the passage of time, from zygote to corpse, as we experience events that unfold in time. From the material world, death is a freeze-frame where motion stops and the organizing force of the material body winks out like a flame. In the totality of That, we always are.

That holds it all: your genealogy, from the first folded proteins to the last human descendant to wear flesh, is eternally extant in full. Depending on your present point of view, death is liberation, or exile, from time. That *is*, always.

There's no more to tell you, since we've reached the borderlands of word and silence, hearing, and experience. When we follow Mystery far enough, we disappear as it disappears.

Encounters with the unknown, with Mystery, carry us away, enrapt us for a time. Each time we taste the ecstasy of vision, we return to our daily lives changed. Each time we touch That, we become a bit more realistic in our views of life, death, truth, love, beauty, pain, and all other sources of Mystery. The point of being born human, in my opinion, is to experience a multiplicity of situations, people, and relationship that teach us the nature of intelligence itself.

Much of experience is painful, difficult, and often deadly. The kind of wisdom we refine from rough experience is a foundation for the kind of wisdom we gather from rapture and ecstasy, a background for understanding, as it were. Without rapturous

vision, life is a grim passage of despair, weakly illumined at times by the satisfaction of survival urges. With the pursuit of Mystery, our perspective grows to include ecstasy with the agony as the extremes of the spectrum of experience.

Life is good, love is good, and wisdom brings peace and balance.

Chapter 18

The Inner Life

Achieving direct experience of That is a hard act to follow. It feels like the only logical and dramatically correct thing to do after returning to normal consciousness is to die. This usually doesn't happen, though, and we're faced with the prospect of years of anticlimax, or so it seems.

The physical world reclaims our attention through bodily needs, family duties, social contacts, and all the details of daily life. As is the practice with earlier raptures, we achieve a working balance through daily meditation sessions. By regularly returning to the experience of That, we enlarge our capacity for enduring its devastating truth.

We also enlarge our capacity of living more fully, for being a better representative of and conduit for Mystery and its truths among our fellow humans. While you're manifesting your individuality on the physical plane, you have certain basic obligations to fulfill, certain work that only you can accomplish. Beyond the generating and/or nurturing of new people, by one means or another, you have the responsibility of elevating the collective self of our species to a more comprehensive level of consciousness. Since this isn't to be done through brute force, you need to learn to offer enlightenment in subtle, attractive ways.

The first order of business is to practice and manifest

Chapter 18 :: The Inner Life

serenity—a condition of balance, competence, and confidence. Serenity should be cultivated from the beginning of your search for Mystery as a means of surviving the experiences of the path. Like most other human qualities and conditions, serenity increases with practice; if you've been working on it from the beginning, it will be in place before and after you experience That. It balances the exaltation of rapture and the intensity of ecstasy with an easy calm in order to allow you to function in daily life and to maintain an appearance of normalcy.

At the beginning of the quest for Mystery, sometimes a person's response to revelation can be extreme. There's an urge to share a stunning realization with other people. I've met some seekers who become manic and obsessed with their new information, who grab their friends by the psychic lapels and launch into semicoherent jabber. The friends then worry about the visionary's sanity, or they grow bored quickly, or both. Other new Mystics become bliss-ninnies, floating with the clouds, oblivious and unearthed, unable or unwilling to pay proper attention to people and things around them. Those with an inflated ego will feel and act superior to people around them. These flawed reactions to Mystery are reasons why the terms "mystic" and "mysticism" are often used as pejoratives.

It's not uncommon for your outer life to become agitated or unstable as you pursue Mystery, and for your own mind to be shaken by the inevitable changes in your views on life, yourself, God, human relationships, and so on. The most important asset you have for achieving and maintaining serenity is a healthy sense of humor. It's applied first to yourself and your situations, and then to other people, to nature at large, and to the flow or the way of things. Humor can manifest as irony—kindly or otherwise—as appreciation of incongruities, serendipities,

Chapter 18 :: The Inner Life

or other surprises; as juxtapositions that somehow make a twisted, but apt, form of sense; of comeuppances and psychic pratfalls.

The first few times that you're swept off your feet by realization's rapture, and then return to bodily consciousness, you no longer fit your former self-image, nor your social mask, nor your psychic skin.

The situation is akin to compressed puberty, and can be as difficult to navigate, no matter what your chronological age. Even though you long for a wilderness hermitage in which to concentrate your time and attention on the pursuit of Mystery, you still have obligations to your own bodily health, to your family, to your creditors, and to your planet. Here are some tips on how to function more smoothly than not.

It helps to add some ritual to your sessions of deliberate pursuit of Mystery, particularly a banishment of your choice. Since banishment is done before and after a rite, the second one can be used to help ground, or earth, yourself, essentially by putting your body and mind in action.

I've always found it helpful to put a pinch of salt in my palm and then lick it. There's something about the sudden, intense taste that hauls my attention back to the material plane quickly. Drink a big glass of water; it seems to start the flow of bodily fluids moving, the sensation of which makes the physical frame a more comfortable place to be.

Do what you can alone before seeking company or companionship. Eat a good meal while your recent revelation sheds its light on the process. Depending on the nature of your realization, contemplate the way the astral energy of the food benefits your astral body, consider the intricate course of metabolism, see the process as "God pouring God into God,"

and so on. Discover how your new truth applies to dining, to doing the dishes, to household chores; discover the Mystery that's been hiding in plain sight all your life. Even walking the dog, changing diapers, or turning a compost pile are acts of Mystery in a mysterious world.

The idea is to integrate the energy liberated by your rapture with your enlarged view of existence, and with your experiences in the material world, profane to profound. The most difficult situations are, as you might expect, those dealing with other human beings. As you see more widely and deeply with each ecstatic revelation, you learn that most people are suffering, and causing, a lot of pain and confusion. If they knew what you know, their attitudes and behaviors would be saner, kinder, and more helpful to themselves and to everyone else.

It should be clear to your expanded vision that a direct approach probably won't work to help or to change people, with the rare exception of those who are ripe for change and Mystery. With the rest, it's wise to maintain, or recreate, a mask of normalcy (whatever that is in your situation) that's reassuring, familiar, and trustworthy. You don't want to alienate anyone through manifest strangeness, since a relatively open and receptive mind is needed for your more subtle approach. The power of silence is often best served by an image of "business as usual."

Once you have saturated yourself and your life with the essence of your most recent vision, you can affect those around you through our Deep Mind connection, through our genetic connection, and by your example of a wiser way of being and of doing things. Action does speak louder than words, especially when the words would be misunderstood or ignored. Your example-giving should flow naturally from situations,

Chapter 18 :: The Inner Life

and should never be accompanied by pointed looks or arched eyebrows.

No matter how many visions we experience, we remain human; our emotional responses to people, events, and memories can shake our equilibrium and evoke feelings and passions so strong that they banish serenity entirely. The old advice about counting to ten before speaking or acting from anger applies to other impulses. Make it a slow count, time your breathing with the count, and recall your most recent realization and the awe and joy it brought to you. Compose your face to display a calm you might not feel yet, pitch your voice lower than distress or agitation would sound, and move slowly. These steps apply when appropriate; there are occasions when strong emotions, immediately expressed, are called for.

You are the proprietor of your emotions; no one else can compel your responses unless you've neglected to learn how to master and manage them. Mastery and management are not suppression and repression, though, but rather recognition and guidance, transmutation and direction. If someone insults you or someone you care for, you have the ability to forego the usual responses of answering in kind or of physical retaliation. If you've integrated the lessons of Mystery into your life, you can maintain a calm and knowing silence.

If a lover betrays you, or justice is denied you, you can decide to save your tears for solitude and keep vengeance for fantasy scenarios. One method of emotional management is to set up a sealed area or chamber in the instinctual part of the astral plane where your imagination constructs situations in which you can allow your emotions full play. Within it, you can satisfy the bloodiest desires of your Forgotten Ones without harm to yourself or to anyone else. This is a temporary, but

useful, way to discharge the forces of your reactions to events. The seal is the most important part of the process, since ideas charged by instinctual power can and probably will manifest in the material plane without it.

Even better, prepare one or more sigils that embody your will to transform yourself through the pursuit of Mystery, then place it or them in the sealed area. When an occasion arises for emotional detonation/demolition, discharge the energy into the sigil(s) to send them into manifestation. A further refinement of employing wild emotions is to use any emotion directed at you by other people in a similar manner. The difference here is that you absorb the energy directly into your sealed chamber and to the waiting sigils. A lack of expected response can inspire new heights of rage or weeping, so you can control, to a certain extent, the length and intensity of another person's emotional outpouring by providing the clues he or she is seeking.

If the rapture-producing vision has demolished previous notions about yourself, your nature, and your place in the world, good. The practice of serenity provides you time and space for adjustment, for settling into your realizations, for remaining alert and aware with an open mind.

Chapter 19

Dark Night of the Soul

The way of Mystery is not an easy, well-marked trail. From the time that you decide to find out for yourself the truth of existence, you work for clues and directions, learning to recognize ever more subtle signs as you go. A good beginning includes reading the works of past Mystics, and of those still living, to get a sense of their experiences and interpretations. If this type of reading isn't an option for you, you can think and remember your life, sifting events for lessons learned and insights achieved.

You can gain ground in your search through methods and metaphors presented in earlier chapters of this book, but your attainments of the knowledge and of the understanding of Mystery are yours alone.

You will encounter dry patches in your journey, times when the Deep Mind seems unreachable and cloaked in silence, when even the memory of rapture fades. Life is full of distracting crises, off-balance relationships, accidents, illness, births, deaths, and taxes. It's during these times that your meditation practice seems useless, but it's even more important than in times when your life is running smoothly.

In a way, spiritual dryness is like catching a cold: it's annoying, uncomfortable, and it handicaps functions of body and mind, but you know from experience that if you wait a

Chapter 19 :: Dark Night of the Soul

week or so, it'll be gone. There are tides beyond blood and ocean that flow in us and around us, and their rhythms bring us ease of, or barriers to, our sense of presence in That.

Different in magnitude and essence from bouts of dryness is what St. John of the Cross calls the Dark Night of the soul.[1]

This condition is a key experience in the course of Initiation, a threshold of destruction, the source of visions of hell. In Roman Catholic terms, one is convinced that God has withdrawn His presence and countenance, abandoning one to complete darkness, sterility, and cold. In nontheistic terms, one is convinced that the intelligence and beauty formerly found in all things has withdrawn its presence and evidence, that stasis reigns, that being itself is complete darkness, sterility, and cold.

It's possible that you began your search for Mystery *after* experiencing the Dark Night; spiritual events happen at inconvenient times and with people in various conditions of awareness. This can appear to be unfair to those who have struggled, in a tradition of grades and degrees, to attain the beginnings of realization and manifestation inch by inch, but such is the way of Mystery.

There are those who arrive at the Dark Night of the Soul through "bottoming out" in alcohol or drug addiction, through the loss of a loved one, through depression and despair. Others find it through a glimpse of the unreality of the world around us, a spontaneous rending of the veil, as it were.

Siddhartha Gotama harvested the Eight Noble Truths from his sojourn in the Dark Night; existence *is* suffering in it. The many-branched way of the Buddha, though, is evidence of the great value of this ordeal. In Christian tradition, the mystery of the agony in the garden speaks of it.

"Then He said to them, 'My soul is deeply grieved, to the

point of death; remain here and keep watch with Me.'

And He went a little beyond them, and fell on His face and prayed, saying, 'My Father, if it is possible, let this cup pass from Me; yet not as I will, but as You will'" (Matt. 26:38–39).[2]

"He went away again a second time and prayed, saying, 'My Father, if this cannot pass away unless I drink it, Your will be done'" (Matt. 26:42).[3]

Self-sacrifice is the essence of the Dark Night of the Soul, not in the sense of leaping into the line of fire to shield someone with your body, nor in the sense of giving yourself to the knives of Aztec priests, but in the sense of surrender to the truth of the self's illusory nature. This surrender is not mere intellectual assent or sentimental agreement, but a profound sundering of parts and distinctions—explosive, scalding, pulverizing.

Everything that you've loved, desired, considered as inspiration, hoped for, believed in, and trusted crumbles under your gaze, disintegrates under your touch. Science and art seem to be shams, based on analyzing and synthesizing temporary configurations of meaninglessness. The Great Work itself, personal transformation, seems both a cruel joke and a useless pursuit. Suicide presents itself as an option, until you realize that killing yourself will neither give meaning to your life and action nor put an end to your misery.

There's a similar, if not identical, state of darkness in the Abyss. This gap in the Qaballistic Tree of Life represents, to me, the boundary between duality and its resolution into nothing. When we begin the quest of truth's mystery, we think in terms relative to our individual selves; how are we to find the truth about ourselves and the universe around us? We consider Mystery, as we consider everything else, to be other than ourselves, a desirable thing "out there."

Chapter 19 :: Dark Night of the Soul

In the lovely curved universe of spirit, if you look far enough, you can see the back of your own head. When the full realization blossoms within you that there's no court of appeals, no external rescue available, that you, yourself, are simultaneously nothing *and* the only game in town, then the Abyss gapes open and in you go. The Dark Night of the Soul seems to be, in large part, the emotional echo or shadow of the Abyss. Abandonment by a parental deity or by an existence that no longer makes sense evokes horror, terror, fear, and dread. It seems to me that the original fear of our more primitive brain layers is the fear of falling. We've been ground-dwellers for a long time now, but I noticed, when my children were infants, a clutch-and-hold reflex when a finger was placed across their palm.

The Abyss can be experienced as a kind of free-fall, with nothing to clutch or hold to break the fall. In the Dark Night of the Soul, the strongest image for me is a desert at night, without stars, moon, or comets, with a gritty, dry surface underfoot. Dealing with the Abyss is an active process of adjustment and rebalance in the midst of drastic change. Dealing with the Dark Night of the Soul is more a process of patience and endurance, faithfully continuing your chosen practices and disciplines without looking for the usual rewards of increased energy and satisfaction.

The Dark Night of the Soul, painful though it may be, is a milestone in the path of Mystery, a reversed rapture, as it were. Instead of being carried aloft in the bliss of ecstasy, one is nailed to the earth, seeing only the physical aspects of things, dismissing spiritual or even astral ways of seeing as meaningless self-delusion. The physical plane proves to be no refuge, though, and one's own mental and emotional health appear uncertain and in peril. There is a spectrum of perception and response in

Chapter 19 :: Dark Night of the Soul

the Dark Night, and your sojourn there will provide you with the full order of it.

Your survival in the realm of spirit depends a lot on your flexibility and elasticity during the Dark Night. If you've linked your identity to a world-view of received truths, whether those of a religious, scientific, artistic, or social faith, their loss could well shatter you instead of dissolving you. If you've staked your existence upon your own identity and its place in the universe, you may reject any proof of your illusory nature, then attempt a return to duality. There is no return to ignorance.

Aleister Crowley called those who failed the Abyss "Black Brothers." This is not a racial designation, but a term describing a spiritual condition. A Black Brother lives in fear of annihilation, in terror of losing his or her identity, and hides from risk and change. In so doing, one also shuts off the influx of energy, prana, and information that one's spirit needs. Life force cannot be conserved or contained, as the flow *is* the force, the movement *is* the energy.

Our spiritual, as well as our physical, topology is that of a tube, not that of a vase or a jar. We flow through our world as our world flows through us, netting and filtering treasures of intelligence, and releasing our own information downstream (and up, if you make a point of it.) If we try to avoid the current of information entering us by sinking attention deep into the effort of preventing alteration to "the way things are," we dam the river of prana, then shrivel of starvation and thirst. If, on the other hand, we seek to retain the influx of energy, to hoard it in order to increase our personal power, we glut and drown.

A Black Brother, like any other Initiate and Adept, sets off to cross the Abyss, to endure the Dark Night of the Soul, but somewhere in that dire passage, courage fails; confidence

Chapter 19 :: Dark Night of the Soul

collapses, and the infant instinct to clutch and grab takes command. What is there to grasp? Scraps of theories, shards of ideas, straws of status and prestige, detritus of discredited faith–useless, and worse than useless, all.

And yet, a Black Brother is still Mystic or Mage, with the knowledge, abilities, and experience necessary to reach the Abyss's brink and the desert's edge. Even from the depths of the Abyss and from the blindness of the Dark Night, a Black Brother can cause havoc around him or her before dwindling away. After damming the flow of the life force at one end or the other, a Black Brother may attempt to steal the life force of others by a variety of means, or to generate astral monsters in the spillage of glut.

Mystery and Magick are ethically and morally neutral in themselves; it's the intent and motives of the individual engaged in either that accomplish help or harm. When you're in the middle of the Dark Night of the soul, it's a good idea to refrain from creative Magick or Mystical pursuit. Banishments and meditations should be performed on schedule, even if you feel no results from either, but anything done to manifest a desire in such a state of confusion and blindness is more likely than not to go wrong.

Eventually, through your perseverance and devotion to practices, the Dark Night will lift with the return of your spiritual vision. In terms of the Abyss, the ashes of your destruction sift into a pyramidal heap on the shore of the great ocean of understanding, after which they're blown back "below" the Abyss to reform in the level to existence that is most akin to your personal nature.

Shadows of the Dark Night of the Soul and of the Abyss are a part of life; people, things, and events in the denser levels of

Chapter 19 :: Dark Night of the Soul

physicality, of emotions and of ideas, multiply and obscure your view of understanding and wisdom. Performing your practices can whisk you through the illusion to restore your point of view to its true condition and size.

How is it possible to lose a vision once you've seen it? The vision remains, but is obscured for us by time-borne events demanding attention and action. A regular, scheduled life with few surprises minimizes demands on your attention, but such a life, in my opinion, is deadly boring. There's a certain rhythm and schedule that our physical bodies maintain, from heartbeat to sleep cycle, that require little supervision by conscious thought. There's a regularity in what we do for a living, a pattern in our dealings with family and friends. Within these layers of order, however, chaos arises with varying degrees of urgency.

The urgencies of life do much to obscure one's memory of Mystery and ecstasy. Emergencies command all of your attention while they're occurring, and it takes time and effort to reduce their presence in memory. If the practices you've chosen work to restore and establish serenity under any circumstances, then you've chosen well. As you regain your calm and your larger range of vision, immediate problems assume their places and their relative gravities in the scheme of things. Coping with other crises in the midst of the most trying of your own, however, is an ordeal of great power.

What gets you through the Dark Night of the Soul? Is it possible to cut short your stay in the Abyss? The only way out is through, and the only way through is dwelling with yourself in serenity. Serenity requires strength, confidence, patience, grace, and compassion. Serenity arises from the vision of No Difference. There is no difference among things, in essence, but only among their forms.

Chapter 19 :: Dark Night of the Soul

In the howling desert wastes of the Dark Night of the Soul, when the illusory nature of things dismays and disgusts you, consider that your identity is yet another illusory thing. We often envision ourselves as gazing, godlike, down upon the chaos and confusion of existence, while at the same time we're in the thick of it ourselves. Once you learn to live with the idea of yourself as an illusion, you have the foundation of serenity. When you can laugh affectionately at the absurdity of everything, the Dark Night lifts.

Although the first time is the most intense, we cross the Abyss on a daily basis, and sometimes more often. The Dark Night of the Soul, once survived, is kept at bay by serenity and by our becoming accustomed to transcending duality regularly. There are times when a serious loss can engender a partial Dark Night, but again, persistence will get you through.

The lifting of the Dark Night of the Soul is a kind of rapture, often slow and subtle, that has no equal among earlier ecstasies. Time has exotic qualities in the Dark Night, and it can feel never-ending, eternal, and damned.

Be assured that it will pass.

Notes:
1. New American Standard Bible.
2. *The Holy Scriptures* (Philadelphia: The Jewish publication Society of America, 1955).
3. Ibid.

Chapter 20

Alone Together

The pursuit of Mystery and the practice of Magick can change your life as few other activities can, for good or ill. Some things that you considered important in the past now seem trivial, and vice versa. You've transformed yourself into a wiser being, a more compassionate person, a more complex entity, and, we hope, into an eager explorer of illusions and realities.

So, what do you do with the rest of your life?

Many of us develop a double life, as it were: we earn a living, belong to a family, have friends of various kinds, and participate in the society around us; at the same time, we live a secret inner life of adventure, peril, and ecstasy. The secrecy arises from the lack of a common vocabulary with those who haven't awakened to the transphysical realms of being, not from any sort of elitism or patronizing attitude. It can be frustrating to think that you're the only person you know who can see what you see and experience what you experience. At the same time, affection, honor, desire, and duty bind you to your "sleepers," both in terms of monetary and emotional support, where applicable, and in terms of assisting their awakening.

The first step in benefiting those you know is to shape your own life according to the realizations you've achieved during the pursuit of Mystery. As you may suspect, this means practicing what you preach (if only silently), doing as you would be done

Chapter 20 :: Alone Together

by, and putting your money where your mouth is—old clichés that speak directly to your situation. Teach by example, by asking questions that are keys to consideration, by answering questions as simply and as clearly as possible. Situations that require a Trickster mode are best operated lightly and without malice.

Even if you're the most fortunate of people in wakening all or most of the sleepers of your acquaintance, they have much to learn that you already know. They need to have their own experiences and ordeals, so be sparing with any help you give. If you consider yourself a playground supervisor (as well as a player) rather than a teacher, you'll be providing the best service you can. At the same time, you can be learning a lot from other people, sleepers or wakers, in terms of viewpoints, information, experiences, and art. Even though you've seen the inner workings of the universe, you're still human; to consider sleepers in any way inferior to you, or to consider yourself to be a great guru, is to invoke a limiting blindness.

Humans are social animals with a long cubhood. We need each other to survive, and this need influences Initiates, Adepts, and Priests during their pursuit of Mystery and Magick. We need shared realities and intelligent conversation, perhaps more with our own generation than with our parents or our children. Often we have to go beyond siblings and the usual outer social groups of work, school, sports, service clubs, and patrons at our favorite watering holes in order to find colleagues. Frequenting the right kind of bookshops and searching the Internet, augmented by an astral call of invitation, can bring you contact with your spiritual sisters and brothers.

You may be surprised at their numbers, especially online. In the first joy of finding colleagues, you may embrace each and

Chapter 20 :: Alone Together

every one as your equal; experience will teach you whom to trust and whom to avoid. There are chains of acquaintance that will lead you to fellow seekers; shared interest and experiences in the Great Work help form bonds easily.

There's no one right way to interact with other people, but I advise that you avoid forming a group with officers and those in permanent leadership positions. When human intelligence operated in a more linear fashion, it made sense to organize groups hierarchically for military and for governing purposes. Esoteric Orders generally adopted the same structure of church and state; several prominent Orders trace their beginnings to the knight-monks of the Crusades.

Today, the most useful pattern of working with a group, in my opinion, is that of a circle of equals in which temporary leadership resides in the person with the most expertise for a given task. Each individual in a group of Mystics and Mages has to show honest and excellent conduct if the group is to become a living and powerful entity in its own right. If one person seems to be going off-balance, his or her colleagues have the duty to listen to the person in order to understand the thinking (or lack of it) behind the words and behavior that indicate a problem. After listening, pondering, and consideration, you can approach the afflicted person in private to discuss the situation.

One of the problems with group work and information exchange among Mystics and Mages is that there is a wide range of perception and understanding, as you have discovered from your own experiences. I've found that the best way to determine another's range of converse is to ask, with full attention and interest evidenced, questions about his or her spiritual adventures and the conclusions about these experiences. This is a subtle drawing-out process, requiring a

Chapter 20 :: Alone Together

light hand. Don't give your opinions unless they're requested; when giving them, avoid any air of superiority (or of inferiority, for that matter).

It is interesting as well as sad that Mystics and Mages can experience trances, visions, and raptures of great truths, yet they sometimes behave like spoiled children. Colleagues often grant more leeway and patience to each other than to those not in the group because of the scarcity of their fellows. You'll have to discover your own limits of tolerance for the obnoxious. When the pain of someone's behavior overbalances the pleasure and usefulness of his or her conversation and company, do what you can to help him or her to change. If the person makes no effort to do so, withdraw your presence.

Other than comparing notes on each other's inner experiences, why should the Mystery-hunters gather with those of like mind and intent? To cite another cliché, "The whole is greater than the sum of its parts." There's a stronger and more emphatic influence on probability from a group than from an individual, generally speaking, unless the individual has a better-placed fulcrum and/or a longer-handled lever, as it were.

Why should a Mystic want to influence probability, one way or the other? Isn't that essentially Magick's business? As I've mentioned on numerous occasions, Magick and Mystery "are two sides of the same coin." "If you're one, you're the other also–but what's the coin that you're both sides of?

Essentially, it's the That with no qualities, the transcendence of duality, the totality of the hologram, the no-thing/nothing, Tao. Each of us is a temporary solidification of free intelligence, distilled for the sake of play and joy, having a hard time sleepwalking in a maze. Waking, we seek each other out, like drops of mercury joining, improving the image of the hologram

Chapter 20 :: Alone Together

by our number. We work to influence probability, to load the dice for the near and distant futures we think most beautiful and appropriate for *genus Homo,* because we can and we must.

Everything in our universe influences everything else, intentionally or otherwise. When you begin your pursuit of Mystery, you influence most directly the rest of the human race through our Magickal link of DNA identification. You influence the other life forms on our planet through the more extensive and more distant links of DNA in general. You change the earth with your footsteps, excavations, and gardening, the atmosphere with your breath, clothing, and bodily movement, the oceans and other waters of the world with the liquids you drink and the fluids you produce. The path of Mystery reveals to you the ways and workings of the world; as you gain information and intelligence (in both meanings of the word) you change, and through your molecular and spiritual links with the rest of us, we change with you.

A Mage and a Mystic are one (and none, of course) person; new information changes understanding and wisdom as it is received, integrated, and absorbed. Since we influence everything whether we know we do or not, to me it seems that as we awaken to the life of the spirit, increasingly we become responsible for directing our influence in a sound and ethical manner. Group work augments individual work in many ways, from the coordination of individual energies in the Great Work to mutual assistance in personal transformation.

You can survive and grow in pursuing Mystery alone; you can't expect a group to do your work for you. Many people join esoteric Orders, covens, and groves in order to learn inner truths in a coherent range of thought, to have the supervision of the more experienced, and to gain the validation of company

Chapter 20 :: Alone Together

on the path. The natural congregation of Mystical peers may provide you with information about others' paths and tips about your own, but since such a gathering isn't a formal teaching organization, just the knowledge that you're not alone in the world is often enough. It's your choice in whom you consider a peer.

It's a good idea to keep your associations in Mystery comfortably loose to prevent a kind of inbreeding and claustrophobia of spirit that can develop among humans. Working together in the realms of Mystery and Magick forms bonds and Magickal links that are difficult to sever, should it become necessary to do so.

That last statement brings up the most problematic of relationships: that between the Mystic and the lover/spouse. There is a variety of scenarios in love relationships in the course of Mystery. When one discovers the way of Mystery as a single person, there's less potential conflict than with another.

When people share a bonding love, there are a number of topics of agreement between them that encourage and bolster the bond. Religion, or its opposite/equivalent, is important to the relationship because of its influence on one's world-view. If people are living in the same house, it's important that they're living in the same universe, as it were, and playing by the same rules. Initiation—the kind that's spontaneously experienced, not the kind that's conferred by an Order—can strike either or both partners, disrupting their current balance of understanding and confidence and confusing their feelings.

If you're the person suddenly aware of transphysical realities, you can, if you're not cautious or in control of your behavior, give the impression that you've gone crazy. It's an easier situation if you and your lover are in the habit of sharing

Chapter 20 :: Alone Together

interesting dreams and creative speculations, but there's still the hazard of fizzing and bubbling emotionally after raptures, often inarticulate and manic. Equally disturbing is the trance of rapture as it's observed by another.

It can be frightening to find your lover's body alive and breathing, but with no presence of attention in it. Attempts to describe visions and transphysical experiences can sound delirious and incoherent.

Two things can help here. The first is open discussion by both parties about events, problems, fears, and trust. The visionary experience is never an excuse for irresponsibility or discourtesy, so you prove your trustworthiness to your partner by keeping agreements and promises. Be even more attentive and gentle with your lover; refrain from conversion attempts—show is better than tell.

The second thing is the establishment of temple space and the mutual honoring of it. When one person is in temple, the other guards its privacy and respects the solitude of the user. Within this sacred space, you can sit entranced, or chant, or dance out new energies free from interruptions. When your lover is similarly engaged, you function as guard and protector. When you're both in temple, you'll notice how the mutual guardianship strengthens the energy vortex within it.

People grow and change at different rates and in different directions. Transformation is a volatile process, and unpredictable. The realm of Mystery is wide and various, and full of paths, from generic paganism to the most complex Ceremonial Magick, to neoshamanism, Wicca, yoga, Buddhism, the Tao, and so on. In a house of good will and respect, choices of different paths shouldn't be divisive. If the relationship is already under a strain or is unbalanced, the pursuit of Mystery

Chapter 20 :: Alone Together

could well be the final straw in its breaking up.

I've seen people flee from the path of Mystery and Magick to take refuge in fundamentalist Christianity; I've seen hostility from a witch for her partner's Thelemic Magick. I've seen a situation where a high priestess of a coven was living with a member of another coven, who wouldn't attend the high priestess' rites. The image of theologians debating how many angels could dance on the head of a pin is no more ludicrous than the sight of Initiates defending their various paths (which ultimately converge, if pursued far enough) as if each had the One True Faith. Perhaps the worst situations I know of involve child custody cases where one parent accuses the other of being unfit because of his or her esoteric beliefs and practices.

When you consider how tangled and painful love relationships can be, it's little wonder that the traditional images of Mystic or Mage show them alone. While it's true that Qaballists of old were required to be married and to be over forty, the conventional ideas of solitude for spirituality have roots in experience.

A solid love relationship can be enhanced, rather than threatened, by one or both partners pursuing Mystery. Ideally, your lover and you are the cosmos for each other, in a Mystical and Magickal sense, without at all excluding the larger existence in which our individuality is imbeded. I've gathered a few principles from years of sometimes painful experiences that may be helpful if there seems to be a conflict between love and Mystery.

- Be courteous and mannerly with your lover; respect his or her spiritual choices and expect similar respect in return.

- Don't diminish the amount of attention that you pay to your lover in order to have more time for your rituals, meditations, or visions. Mystery will provide enough time for you; don't be greedy for rapture.

- If your lover asks you to describe your visions and your ecstasies, it would be no lie to be as artistic as possible with the former, nor to assure him or her that the ecstasy is akin to that found in your lovemaking.

- If your lover wants to pursue Mystery as you do, guided meditations can be helpful. With words, lead the way in revisiting your visions, letting your voice fade to silence at the proper times. Afterward, conversation and a good meal help to ground the energies.

- Share your library and such notes as you choose, but don't try to do your lover's work for him or her.

- If your lover chooses another way to mystery than your own, be supportive. Discuss the signs of predatory cults and controlling gurus. Any group that demands secrecy from a mate or lover is dangerous and should be avoided.

- Conversion attempts between lovers are essentially power struggles. Don't even try it.

- Use what you learn in your visions to direct your own transformation in the way your nature requires. Be wise and kind in this art, and don't aim at impressing, intimidating, or dom-

Chapter 20 :: Alone Together

inating your lover. We all change and grow, but not necessarily in the same direction.
- The search for Mystery often shatters toxic or unhappy relationships. The more you see, the less you can make excuses for another's bad behavior. Liberation is often painful.

As for relationships with parents, siblings, and other relatives, play them as they are. Many times, parents often feel like the hen who hatched a duck egg as they watch their offspring develop into unique humans who explore new realms of idea, philosophy, and behavior. Everything you are genetically came through your parents to you: for this they deserve honor, but not unquestioning capitulation to their tastes and opinions.

Siblings sometimes share interests, but often there's a divergence among them from early childhood. Again, your situation is unique, and only you can decide how much to share and how much to keep in silence with them and with other relatives.

Rather than seeing your daily life and its obligations as an annoyance and a distraction from the pure pursuit of Mystery, or seeing your time in transcendence as a guilty pleasure, live them both seamlessly and without conflict as they eventually blend. If someone in your environment is making this difficult to do, examine your situation closely and make the necessary decisions. There's no dishonor in cloaking your inner life in silence and discretion should the need arise. If a religious fundamentalist demands to know what you're doing, say that you're at prayer. If parents question your times of solitude, let them know that you're seriously considering your options for the future.

Since the way of Mystery includes aspects of both, you're

Chapter 20 :: Alone Together

not misspeaking. It doesn't take much experience in dealing with other people to learn what you can say to whom, and what you can't. With a little thought and consideration of the factors of your environment, you can achieve the peace you need. There are times when silence isn't just the wise course of living, but is also the most compassionate.

Chapter 21

The View From Now

There's not much more that words can do to share with you the Mystical and Magickal experiences available to the determined seeker. I've been walking, running, crawling, and flying in pursuit of the ineffable for about sixty years now, and I've sculpted a reality from what I've learned that makes sense (to me) and provides a measure of, purpose for, and satisfaction in, living.

As I've mentioned, one of the "Maxims of Maat" is: whatever is, lives; whatever lives is intelligent. Harking back to the anthropic principle that I cited at the beginning of this book, the idea that the universe exists because we're here to observe it is a bit silly, considering how little we observe ourselves and the ecology of our own planet and how short the time has been that we've existed as a species. If we expand the concept of "we," however, to include everything that can observe, it begins to make more sense. Human chauvinism limits our perceptions and our thinking and keeps us in a state of adolescent self-reference.

The instant when manifestation began remains a Mystery. Undifferentiated young matter could only be dimly aware of itself, but its awareness was sufficient for observation of gravity variations and the formation of thicknesses within itself. It was with the formation and ignition of stars that observation of more detail could occur. First generation stars observed each

Chapter 21 :: The View From Now

other through gravity and radiation, as well as through their unity at the beginning. Theirs was a simple awareness that increased in complexity with the formation of heavier elements within them and the space that grew among them. In their dying explosions they enriched the next generation of suns, the planetary belts of those suns, and the life arising on the planets that formed from the belts. The death and birth of stars in fire I see as an event of which the Phoenix is a symbol and image.

Second generation stars not only observe; they think and communicate via their plasma flow and convection currents that code meaning into their radiation, and receive information through a coronal perceptive field. Original unity and gravity also provide connection among them. Planets, asteroids, comets, and the life arising on them, developed, and are still developing, consciousness in various degrees of sophistication. Consciousness is a complex and chaotic pattern of flows that recognizes and understands itself, no matter the extremes of form in which it arises and in which it is seated.

I learned this in vision trances, in raptures of visceral presence, a condition in which the physical body responds to transphysical events and information. Excitement and anticipation is balanced by utter calm and awareness as attention is focused on the vision's event; the situation gave rise, in my opinion, to the phrase, "bated (abated) breath." The aim, in such situations, is to observe and record without judgment, analysis, or commentary. What I know about the consciousness of stars is what the stars tell me and show me in vision trance (and occasionally without the formality).

In general, stars with planetary systems have more interest in organic life than stars without planets. Not all stars are sane or benevolent. Stars vibrate like gongs or bells, and each

Chapter 21 :: The View From Now

has its signature chord, with overtones, shading, and all. Our own sun is one of the organizers of the Comity of the Stars, whose purpose is to foster and protect emerging life in its various forms, wherever it arises. The protection doesn't extend to environmental competition, food-chain position, or the occasional catastrophic asteroid strike, but concerns itself with deliberate predation, destruction, or slavery from sources external to the young life form's habitat.

At our current stage of development as a species, stellar doings aren't a concern of ours, except on the physical level of astronomy, astrophysics, and space technology. On an individual and transphysical level, stellar conversation can be quite interesting; reach out your mind and listen intently for meaningful, wordless song. I mention the sentient stars and their comity's purpose since an invitation awaits us to participate in it, once we've achieved the maturity of our second consciousness. It's one of the things for us to do when we grow up.

In other trances I've met N'Aton, the self-named persona of our next level of magnitude in consciousness. It could well be that you've already met it/us under another name, or perhaps have mistaken him/her/them for Jesus. The essence of both Jesus and N'Aton is solar, beautiful, and charismatic, but Jesus is a spiritual savior incarnated in our past, according to the official legend, and N'Aton is a state of consciousness we're working to attain. On another level, they *are* each other, but for our purposes here we're treating time as linear. Encountering either in meditation or trance can produce the sweetest of raptures and an ecstatic sense of rebirth.

On the other hand, some people consider a state of double consciousness and the connections of information-flow it

Chapter 21 :: The View From Now

enables to be a dystopian scenario of totalitarian control over the individual. In my experience, which occurs, for the most part, in levels less dense than the physical, the species consciousness is a background presence of white noise to individual thinking most of the time. Information rises from it for your attention and according to your interest in various topics and when there are species-wide issues to consider. In many ways, the double consciousness resembles the Internet without hardware; there are times when the Internet seems like training wheels for N'Aton, as it were.

I've been asked whether N'Aton is the same as the Omega Point. This concept, which I first encountered in the writings of Pierre Teilhard de Chardin, seems to mean the transcendence of the physical plane as a species. N'Aton is seated in the physical bodies and mental structures of its participants, and will remain so for an unspecified time. With further development of genetic engineering, we'll be adapting ourselves for environments now closed to us. Our interconnection in N'Aton will not only keep communication open, but will tend to keep us all essentially human, no matter how extreme the forms.

Genetic engineering is a marvelous closed loop of self-reference. DNA has determined our shape and abilities from our emergence as a species, and now we're beginning to make small changes in the shape and abilities of DNA. There are those among us who hold that such changes are evil, and against the will of God. Others hold that a capacity is both license and encouragement, and argue that if God/DNA didn't want us to explore, He/She/It wouldn't have given us curiosity, dexterity, and intelligence. My own take on it is that it's a humorous situation, much funnier than the legend of the Fall in Eden, and will probably teach us the limits of our scientific intelligence.

Chapter 21 :: The View From Now

N'Aton is a step, a stage, in human development; what lies beyond I haven't seen directly, but I do know that there *is* a "beyond." It will be an order of magnitude more complex and extensive than N'Aton, but more than that I can't say.

What of individuality, personhood, and identity in a state of double consciousness? They remain, with a new maturity, as do group affiliations of various kinds. Maturity includes practicing what you preach, keeping your word, respecting wisdom, and putting love to work. Individual identity, secure in its larger context of species participation, develops in confidence, with fewer traumas and scars to twist its growth than we have in our unlinked present. Our collective consciousness doesn't hold all the answers to Mystery and it doesn't prevent Magick or mistakes.

What it does allow is a type of managed reincarnation, where a discarnate individual can maintain its unique pattern of consciousness through the friendly memories of the living until such time as a zygote is created for its return to the physical world. This often happens within family lines, where it encourages intergenerational courtesy and respect for obvious reasons. For those who have had enough of identity, it's possible to decline reincarnation in favor of dissolution into the cosmos. Dissolution does not erase the treasures of your discoveries and accumulated wisdom. The harvest of a life is shared among the living, enshrined in the common consciousness, long after the harvester disappears.

There are other states of consciousness after death, shaped by the beliefs one dies with; there are heavens, hells, purgatories, paradises, Edens, and others that serve as schools. In them, people learn that their visions of eternal bliss or torture soon grow boring and banal. They learn that a "God"

Chapter 21 :: The View From Now

whose reward for a good and faithful life consists of singing praises to and about Him is an egomaniac who had to create a fan club. They learn that a "devil" whose punishment for sin consists of applying pain in all conceivable ways is just the back of God's head, a false face of duality.

The nature of individual consciousness isn't a simple thing, nor is it subject to universal definition. One of my visions concerns "the plane (or plain—it fits the topography) of the unborn," where reincarnating spirits oversee the development of the fetuses that will be their bodies. The image is of a gently rolling, grassy landscape dotted with glowing nests that resemble heaps of rainbow cotton candy; in the nests are the incoming souls who resemble golden ostrich eggs. This sounds disgustingly precious, but it's what I saw. What I learned here, and in similar vision-locales, is that there is no fixed moment for the appearance or departure of the soul, intellect, or personhood among us.

Those who are reincarnating after lifetimes of experience generally wait to ensoul at birth, at first feeding, or even later. Since there are more bodies coming into existence than there are seasoned individualities to inhabit them, we have the presence of "first-time elementals" among us, individuals formed from the natural development of zygote into embryo into fetus into child and beyond. First-timers are often physically beautiful, intelligent, charismatic, and amoral. They're self-referential in the extreme, and may take several rounds in and out of flesh to learn consideration of other people, animals, plants, and relationships.

There are developmental disorders of the spirit, some of which are linked to physical problems, that produce human-seeming monsters. Denizens of the lower astral planes can and

Chapter 21 :: The View From Now

do invade a developing body to take control of it in various degrees, especially if the mother's protective field is damaged by her responses to a toxic situation. We already know about some of the physical effects on a developing human body that can be damaged by maternal alcohol ingestion, her exposure to harmful radiation, chemical dumps, bad diet, and so forth. If she's living with psychological abuse, abandonment, poverty, and other stresses, the normal pregnancy response of love and protection can be stripped away or poisoned, and the new life is vulnerable, open to invasion.

One thinks of Hitler, Caligula, Stalin, Pol Pot, Jim Jones, Idi Amin, and others of the same stripe as obvious examples of a combination of lower astral invasion and first-time-elementalhood. These individuals gained great power through their elemental intelligence and charisma, and used it to cause great suffering and death. There are similar people who lack the power of the famous ones, but whose behavior causes suffering and death in their families and in individual victims. If the opponents of abortion investigated the realities of the astral and spiritual planes instead of relying on the opinions of the Bible's authors and their present-day interpreters, maybe they would realize how their own zeal guarantees the birth of moral monsters to unwilling and unhappy mothers. Then again, maybe not.

Occasionally, our species produces geniuses, people of extreme talent in at least one field. They seem to be "throw-forwards," people who are double-conscioused in a single- or semi-conscious world. Some are multiple incarnators, some are favorable mutations, but all are from human stock. Some geniuses are gifted in one field of human ability and deprived in others, such as the so-called idiot savants who can calculate

Chapter 21 :: The View From Now

large numbers, memorize statistics, or repeat perfectly music they've heard only once, but can't keep themselves alive without supervision. Brain and mind work together to fashion themselves over a period of time; most instances of precocious, arrested, or skewed development have a physical base that will prove correctable as medical science learns more.

The visions cover other topics. We've been dealing with nonhuman entities, Deep Mind, and divine intelligence throughout our history and prehistory, from which grew many a legend and myth. The Ages of Faith and Reason instituted diabolism and denial in the names of religion and science, but those who have experienced, know. *What* we've seen, however, has varied according to the generally accepted world-view of the seers, and their reports reflect their belief systems. Who, or what, are these Others?

For a long time, they were interpreted as nature spirits and ancestors, then as gods, angels, saints and djinn, ghosts, faeries, and aliens from outer space. I've learned to discount specific forms in visions, except as they add detail to the information being received. The public miracles of Fatima, Lourdes, and other manifestations of Mary, mother of Jesus are the closest the Church comes to recognizing the power of the feminine principle, indicates the power to affect perceptions, behavior, and health held in and by that principle. Crowds at visitation/apparition sites form a group mind based on hope and devotion, a mind hungry for "proof" of the existence of Mystery, albeit in the form or forms it knows and expects.

The universe we know is a living thing, and so are the universes that we don't know. Our experience of time is partial, constrained by our present capacities of perception and understanding, seemingly linear and unidirectional. The

Chapter 21 :: The View From Now

Others that are occasionally reported among us have a more complete grasp of both time and space than we do presently, and can enter and leave our world at will, as it were. They're as real as we are, though after a different fashion, and whatever information they communicate to us may or may not be useful to us in our present state. In this sense, N'Aton is an Other, but he/she/it is all us, human to the core.

I've learned that we have everything we need to become what we're supposed to be. Those who insist that we need the wisdom and/or technology of star-brother-aliens in order to survive are just pining for a messiah in science-fiction drag. There is no *deus ex machina* waiting to swoop down from the sky to save our bacon for us, on the physical plane or on any other.

There are Magickians I've met who claim that in the future there is no Malkuth on the Tree of Life, that we'll all be pure spirit in a spirit world. On the contrary: the physical plane is necessary to our form of consciousness; its beginning and its development have shaped us, and will continue to shape us. We are Adam, the red earth, formed from the dust of stars, who took our own first breath by means of the way things work. We needed no Godly breath to animate us, nor were half of us derived from a rib from the other half. The physical plane is to be loved, not disdained as somehow inferior to spirit.

When I was a child I saw a Gypsy funeral in a cemetery near our house. Instead of wearing the customary black of mourning, all were brightly dressed, a band was playing, and the attitude was celebratory. After retrieving my younger brother who wanted to join them, my father told me that he'd heard that Gypsies celebrate at funerals because the deceased's troubles were over at last. Both life and death are phases of existence

Chapter 21 :: The View From Now

that hold pleasure and pain. Neither is a real escape from the other, and both are illusions, ultimately.

What, if anything, does it all mean? Is there a point to the causing change to occur in conformity with will that is Magick? Is there a point to expanding one's vision through the raptures of Mystery? Is there a destiny for us, individually and collectively, greater and holier than producing and educating successive generations of humans at the behest of our DNA?

My best answer is yes. Our existence charges us with the task of learning to love, to expand our understanding and wisdom about everything around us and within us, to grow more complex, sophisticated, strong, and compassionate. The loves we experience in childhood, in religion, in mating, in parenthood, in aging, and in dying are hints and reflections of the great love that calls us to dissolve within it, always and everywhere.

This great love is not easily won, as it requires a transformation within each of us from living by instinct and rationalization to living according to our unity with all of existence and with That beyond existence. Further difficulties arise from living among other people who content themselves in living from instinct, and often from unbalanced instinct at that, and who count love as a weakness.

Great love has no fear of death, of being killed, or of killing when necessary. Great love is usually moved to protect the disadvantaged from bullies, crooks, and abusers, when appropriate; great love also knows when to mind its own business and let others learn from experience. It holds with the golden rule of "Do unto others as you would have them do unto you," with the Wiccan Rede of "An ye harm none, do what ye will," with the Law of Thelema of "Do what thou wilt shall be

Chapter 21 :: The View From Now

the whole of the law; love is the law, love under will." With full realization, love and will become the same thing.

When your nature is transformed by wisdom into a living love, you treasure beauty, truth, and nobility of heart wherever and whenever you encounter them. You come to appreciate innocence, honesty, loyalty, and all the other virtues that humans hold as ideals. You also learn to be severe and decisive when necessary, to use guile and wile, to be a Trickster when appropriate. You laugh, weep, and feel deeply, all while working tirelessly to open ways for other people to approach their own transformations in Magick and Mystery.

Our Golden Age lies ahead of us, not behind us; just what we'll become is an unknown, but it's an *unknown,* a Mystery to be pursued, not feared.

Don't take my word for it–see for yourself.

N'ATON

Visions of the Major Arcana

The Tarot is an ancient book of wisdom, a book of pictures rather than words, clues rather than statements. It is used for divination or fortune telling in its popular, or Outer aspect. On the Inner, the Tarot links with the Tree of Life and the Zodiac. The individual cards function as mandalas and talismans; the deck as a whole provides a secret language of the Unconscious and a higher consciousness.

This deck is named the N'Aton Tarot in honor of that which we are becoming.

N'Aton is the persona of the new human species, *Homo veritas*. *Homo veritas* is distinguished from *Homo sapiens* by a double consciousness: that of the individual and that of the species. The species consciousness is Jung's Racial Unconscious in an awakened state. It manifests in the individual as a background awareness of all other individual humans as well as the tides of consensus which are N'Aton's thinking.

Strong signals can arise from the background awareness to alert all to conditions of danger, distress or pain. If one lacks food, all feel hunger; if one plots murder, all would know.

The individual is aware of the responses to his or her behavior, speech and personality. Insight and self-knowledge can be aided tremendously by seeing ourselves as others see us. When we are N'Aton, there will be no war, violence, neglect, cruelty, or prejudice.

This Tarot is being fashioned to assist and accelerate our species' transformation. The trumps are drawn from many cultures, many ages. They invoke the various Aeonic formulae, traditions of practice, and stages of philosophy that comprise Magick: the Science and the Art of causing change to occur in conformity with Will.

The mutation into *Homo veritas* is the first such change that we can consciously attain. These trumps are clues to various methods of becoming a new kind of human being. The transformation can only be done to oneself by oneself. Information is helpful, love and support are priceless–but in this, we are each our own Messiah.

Onward to adventure!

THE FOOL *(Aleph)* is the Innocent, the wanderer, the third brother in the fairy tales. He travels far, questing as Parsifal for the Grail, expanding the boundaries of experience since he knows nothing of limits. He goes as far as his technology will take him.

Adjustment *(Lamed)* is the equilibrium of the universe in motion. In Egyptian terms she is Maat: truth, righteousness, balance, and the correct establishment of boundary lines. In the Hall of Judgment, Anubis balances the heart of the deceased with the feather of Maat. If the heart is innocent and light as a feather, the soul proceeds to the blessed land of Amenta.

Together they are AL, the Hidden God. They are Chaos and Order, which are mutually necessary for the harmony and variety of life. As AL, they are the purest expression of love under will.

    The Magus *(Beth)* employs his knowledge of the ways of nature to accomplish deeds that seem miraculous to others. He speaks his Word and the universe is transformed by the Magickal Current which his will directs.

    The Star *(He')* is the Magickal Current used by the Magus. The essence of the Star flows into the vessels prepared for it and then flows into the world, nourishing life and elevating consciousness. The Star is pure energy.

    Together, the Magus and the Star are Magick at work. Wisdom needs power in order to change things; power needs direction in order to have an effect.

    The Priestess *(Gimel)* is responsible for the connection of the human and the divine in nature. She is the leader of the Mysteries, the dancer of ritual, the keeper of the temple. She invokes the gods, not so much to manifest their power through her, but to demonstrate to others how they might invoke themselves.

    The Hierophant *(Vau)* is responsible for the connection of the human and the divine within oneself. He guides the Initiation process, including the Ordeals that are part of it. Ordeals are the karma incurred and discharged in the process of radically changing one's consciousness through Initiation.

    Together, they are the balanced formula for spiritual progress: work on the Outer and work on the Inner, group ritual and solitary rites, participation and realization. Initiation is ultimately self-directed: each Initiate must learn to use the

power of the gods and to anticipate Ordeals in order to avoid them. Ordeals can be avoided by correcting one's spiritual condition voluntarily and promptly.

The Empress *(Daleth)* embodies the female energies raised to their highest level of responsibility and the fulfillment of duty and function. She represents the Vegetable Kingdom of earthly life, the nurturing mother aspect of the Goddess and the bountiful harvest. She is linked with Venus and can be a doorway into love and creativity.

The Emperor *(Tzaddi)* symbolizes the male energies raised to the highest level of responsibility and the fulfillment of duty and function. He represents the Animal Kingdom of earthly life, the providing father aspect of the God, the productive hunt and husbandry. He is linked with Aries, springtime, new beginnings, and the power of fire.

Together, the Empress and Emperor present the dignity of power used with compassion and love. They speak of humanity's responsibility for the welfare of and right relationship with Nature in all her forms. Humanity is the neurosystem of planet Earth, the cephalic director of the biosphere, the brain through which the mind and soul of terrestrial Nature seeks to increase intelligence. Only in this responsibility does humanity deserve the title "Crown of Creation."

The Chariot *(Cheth)* is a symbol of the soul's progress on the path of Initiation, an image of motion and of GO-ing. (Some say the card is better titled "The Charioteer.") The letter Cheth means "fence." At first thought this seems to contradict the

image of GO-ing, but roadside fences can be useful in preventing wrong turnings.

Fortune *(Kaph)* is the wheel of Karma, in which Justice can manifest in the guise of Chance. To avoid the snares of triumph and despair, one should seek to abide in the hub rather than on the rim.

Together, these wheeled cards represent change and progression, the activity of linear and temporal vision. Attempting to stand still is futile; there is no turning back. Wisdom says to guide the course of travel and enjoy the ride.

The Hermit *(Yod)* is the individual consciousness, the singular point of view. It is the fertilizing spermatozoa, the minute packet of information that unites with the surrounding universe to produce a new being. The Hermit of the New Aeon does not live in isolation, but rather in integrity amid chaos and the lures of *Maya*.

Lust *(Teth)* is the process whereby the union takes place. It is the great yearning for completion that renews earthly life generation after generation, and infuses the individual with zest and appreciation for all that lives. Lust is the drive to unity with the All/Nothing, the urge that is the motive for seeking Initiation and adhering to the Path.

Together, the Hermit and Lust comprise the dynamic tension of self and Other, solitude and intimacy, autonomy and unity. Both sperm and egg disappear in the creation of the zygote. This is the dissolution whereby one crosses the Abyss.

The Hanged Man *(Mem)* is one of the most mysterious trumps in the Tarot. He is hanging by his foot, not his neck, so the idea of execution or violent death is not the image's intention. His is the principle of undertaking Ordeals or discipline (as in Yoga) in order to gain Spirit Vision.

Death *(Nun)* is a major transformation in the human experience. It represents, Alchemically, the process of putrefaction or composting, whereby organic remains are made useful for the growth of new life. The Baron Samedhi not only rules the dead and presides over cemeteries, but is also Lord of the Crossroads.

Together these cards represent discipline and wise choice, the training and transformation of the Initiate, the difficulties and the termination of life. Experience in Magick brings the sure knowledge that Death is but another Great Initiation.

The Devil *(Ayin)* is surprise, the unexpected. Like the Judeo-Christian Yahweh, the Devil is thought to be a single, male entity. Devil=Double=Duality; the Goddess and the Horned God together create the power of Pan, Cernunos and Herne as well as the power of Aradia, Cerridwen, and Bridgid. It is the procreative power of desire.

The Tower *(Pe)* is destruction, obliteration, annihilation, Shivadarshana. It is in the resolution of duality in the awareness of the illusory nature of self-identity. Pe means "mouth", an important organ in Maat Magick.

The Tower and the Devil together give the gist of an Initiation Ordeal, even unto the crossing of the Abyss.

The Moon *(Qoph)* is viewed from space by an "outlandish" group of people. Some astronomers deem our Moon a sister planet who forms a binary unit with the Earth, rather than a mere satellite like Phobos or Deimos. The large reflecting surface of the Moon lights the night for woodland revels, faerie dances and altar-stone rituals. As the nearest and most influential of heavenly bodies (excepting the Sun), the Moon is the most logical physical goddess.

The Sun *(Resh)* is shown at its rise, honored by a pagan people. Science has demonstrated that all life on Earth depends on the Sun's energy. There is no more logical physical god for this planet than the Sun.

The Moon and the Sun represent the fundamental earthly archetypes of opposites: light and darkness, day and night, active and passive.

Art *(Samech)* Art's alchemical symbols are the lion and eagle, and its method of operation is that of the arrow shot from the bow. This aligns with Art's astrological attribution of Sagittarius, the Archer. The rainbow is a stage of alchemical process and veils a certain Mystery.

The Lovers *(Zain)* are Shiva and Kali, bearing swords (Zain), which are weapons of Air and are linked with Gemini, the astrological attribution of the card. Their alchemy is the union of opposites in 2–0.

Art and The Lovers are the two primary alchemical cards among the trumps. In this case, the pair is depicted in American

Indian and Hindu imagery.

The Aeons *(Shin).* The traditional Last Judgment trump was transformed into the Aeon by Aliester Crowley. In the light of recent Magickal events, this card has been expanded into The Aeons. In depicting each Aeon in its respective godform, the card illustrates that all Aeonic formulae are in practice somewhere in the world now.

The Universe *(Tau)* is imaged as the Black Pearl in the Crystal Lotus. The Lotus is presented by Metatron, Angel of Kether, for the Initiate to hold. This assures us that as we are contained by the universe, so the universe is contained in us.

Together, these trumps are Time and Space, the continuum in which we live, perceive, and think. The cards suggest ways in which we might transcend the limits of Space and Time as we know them. Magick works through the quantum plane to influence probability in accordance with Will. Through the effective use of Magick, we become able to do things formerly attributed to angels or gods.

To view the paintings that follow in full color please visit the
Black Moon Art Gallery:

BlackMoonPublishing.com/gallery

N'ATON

N'ATON :: Visions of the Major Arcana

FOOL

N'ATON :: Visions of the Major Arcana

ADJUSTMENT

N'ATON :: Visions of the Major Arcana

PRIESTESS

N'ATON :: Visions of the Major Arcana

HIEROPHANT

![Empress illustration]

EMPRESS

EMPEROR

CHARIOT

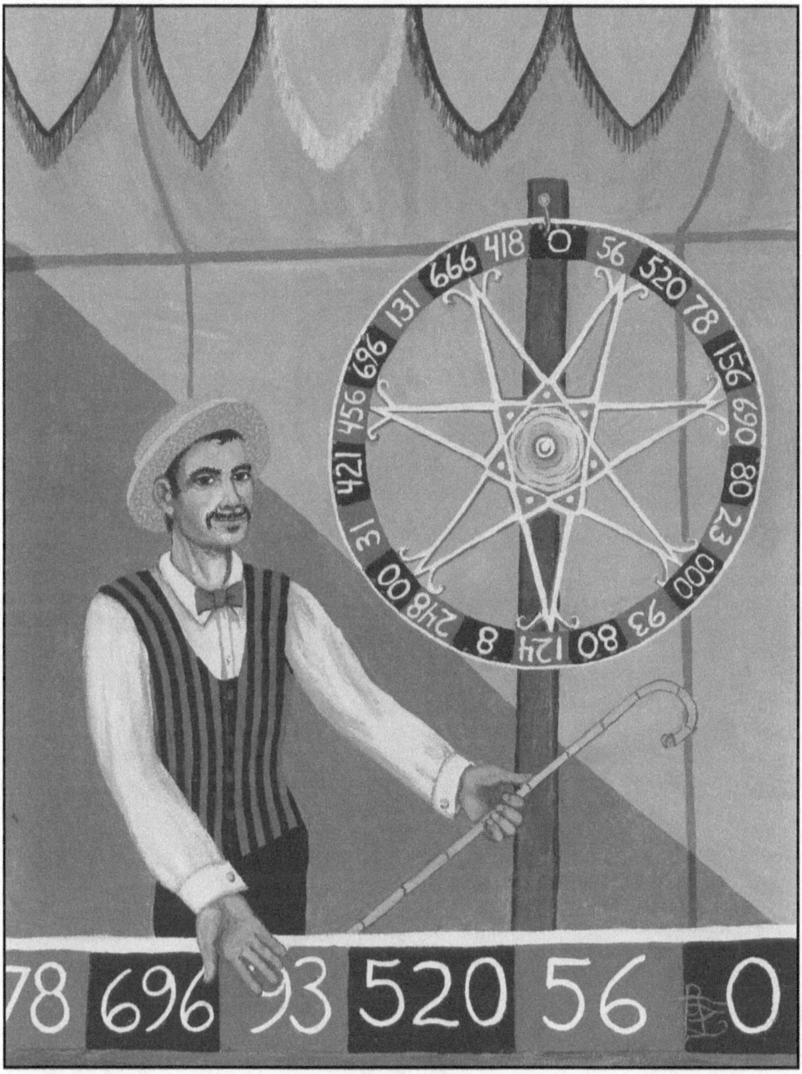
418
0
56
520
78
156
690
80
23
000
93
80
124
8
248
00
31
421
456
696
131
666
78 696 93 520 56 0

FORTUNE

HERMIT

LUST

![Hanged Man illustration]

HANGED MAN

DEATH

DEVIL

N'ATON :: Visions of the Major Arcana

TOWER

THE MOON

THE SUN

N'ATON :: Visions of the Major Arcana

![Art illustration]

ART

LOVERS

N'ATON :: Visions of the Major Arcana

THE ÆONS

N'ATON :: Visions of the Major Arcana

UNIVERSE

N'ATON :: Visions of the Major Arcana

STAR

N'ATON :: Visions of the Major Arcana

MAGUS

Appendix A

This is the document that filtered through my awareness and my hand from a vision after a group time-travel Working in 1974. It's the base of my system of Maat Magick, and its language and style reflects the books and practices in which I was immersed at the time.

Liber Pennae Praenumbra

1. In the Akasha-Echo is this inscribed:

2. By the same mouth, O Mother of the Sun, is the word breathed forth and the nectar received. By the same breath, O Counterweight of the Heart, is the manifest created and destroyed.

3. There is but one gate, though there appear to be nine, Mime-dancer of the Stars. How beautiful thy weft and web, a-shimmering in the fire-dark of space!

4. The two that are nothing salute you, Black Flame that moves Hadit! The less and less One grows, the more and more Pra-NU may manifest. Do thou now speak to us, the children of the time-to-come; declare thy will and grant thy Love to us!

5. THEN SPAKE SHE THAT MOVES:

6. I hurl upon ye, Children of Heru! All ye who love the Law and keep it, keeping Naught unto yourselves, are ye a-blest. Ye have sought the scattered pieces of Our Lord, ceasing never to assemble all that has been. And in the Realm of the Dead have ye begotten from the Dead the Shining One. Ye then gave birth, and nourished Him.

7. Thy Land of Milk shall have the honey also, dropped down as dew by the Divine Gynander. The pleasure and delight lie in the Working, the Whole surpassing far the Parts together.

8. The Lord of Parts is placed within his kingdom, as done by Beast and Bird. The land of Sun is open but to Children. Heed the Eternal Child – his Way is flowing-free, and suited to the Nature of your being.

9. A Voice crieth in the Crystal Echo:

10. What means this showing-forth? Is Time Itself awry? The Hawk has flown but threescore and ten in His allotted course!

11. She smiles, as beauteous as Night:

12. Behold, He spreads His pinions yet in flight, showering and shaking forth the Golden Light upon the hearts of men. And wherein doth He fly, and by what means? The Feather and the Air are His to ride, to bear him ever in his GO-ing.

13. The pylons of the ages are unshaken, firmly are they Set.

The Day of the Hawk has but seen its dawning, and will see its due measure according to the Laws of Time and Space.

14. The Voice then spoke:

15. Then has the Vision failed? Do I behold Thee crookedly, thinking Thee to be Whom Thou art Not?

16. She danced and whirled, scattering starlight in her silent laughter.

17. I Am Whom I appear to be, at times, and then again I wear a triple veil. Be not confused! Above all, Truth prevails.

18. I am the Unconfined. Who is there to say me nay, to say, Thou shalt not pass."? Who indeed may say, Thy time is yet to come," when Time itself is my chief serving-maid, and Space the Major-domo of my Temple?

19. Indeed, O Voice of the Akasha, I am the means by which you speak. By the same mouth that breathes the Air, do words of doubt pour forth. In silence then, do know Me. For I am come with purpose at this time, to aid the Lovers of the Hawk to fly.

The Word of Flight

20. Who falters in the Flight must thereby fall: the greatness of the Gods is in the GO-ing.

21. When first ye fledged, Beloved of Heru, the shell which

had protected long had broken. Upon the Wings of Will ye ventured forth, gaining strength and power as ye flew. Ye gained all knowledge of the Feathered Kingdom, whereby ye became as perfect as the Sun. The friends and teachers all became as brothers.

22. The regal Swan, the Heron and the Owl – the Raven and the Cockerel did aid ye. The Beauty of the Hawk Himself was granted, the virtues of the Peacock, the Hummingbird and Loon. The Eagle did reveal her inner nature and the mysteries thereof – behold, ye witnessed how, with her Lion, she became the Swan. And the Ibis of the Abyss did show the Knowledge.

23. Ye flew, O Kings and Hermits! And ye fly even now, within the bending loveliness of NU. But there are those among ye, and below ye, who would snare your wings and drag ye from the sky.

24. Look well within! Judge well your Heart! If ye be pure, it weighs no more than 1. It will not bear ye down to the Abyss. For Gold is Light, but Lead is fatal unto flying – plumb your own depths, in Truth and in self-knowledge.

25. If aught would hinder thee, it is thy doing. Behold this teaching now within the Temple.

26. So saying, She-Who-Moves assumed the form of the great Black Flame, growing from the central shaft and billowing out into the Void. The Children of Heru beheld in silence, and listened to Her words form in their hearts.

27. Behold! This lens of Stars now turning in Space before ye – men have named it well Andromeda. Through it I flow unto the holy Moondog, and thence to Ra, and thence to ye, O Priests.

28. Ye must not rest content whilst in the Kingdom, but strive and so exceed in what is done. In Love of the Lady of the North, and in Will of the Prince of the South, do every thing soever. In the power of the Seven-rayed Star do ye comprehend the Beast. And from HAD of the Heart do delight in thy star-arched darling.

29. Do all this, and then, pass beyond. Abandon aught that might distinguish thee from any other thing, yea, or from no-thing. If the fowler would snare thee, leave thy feather-cloak a-dangle in his hand and soar naked and invisible beyond!

30. But now! As priests within the Temple are ye here, as Kings, and Warriors, Magickians all. The Way is in the Work.

31. The Hidden One of the Abyss now gives the two wherein is wrought the higher Alchemy: supporting Earth is Chthonos – learn it well, and all bonds shall be loosed for the Will's Working. Surmounting Spirit, there is Ychronos, whose nature is duration and the passing-away thereof.

32. The two are one, and form the Kingdom's essence. Who masters them is Master of the World. They are the utter keys of Transmutation, and keys of the power of the other Elements.

33. The Warrior-Priests received the Keys, and placed them within their robes, to hold them hidden well above their hearts. The Black Flame danced and dwindled, becoming small, a quill pen, plumed and pointed. There being naught upon which to write, one among the Priests came forth, and laid his body's skin upon the altar as living parchment.

34. She-Who-Moves wrote thereupon a Word, but shew it not before them. In patience waited all the Kings and Hermits, assured full well of final Understanding.

35. The Feather grew again, and rounded close its edges, becoming to their eyes the Yonilingam. The image came of Ancient Baphomet, the Horned One, who spoke:

36. Of old ye knew the Key of Two-in-One conjoined. Ye have lived and loved full measure as NU and HAD, as PAN and BABALON. The Mystery of mine own image do ye also know, for such a Truth was for the ancient Orders of the East and West.

37. Bipartite has the Race of Man been in its span. The Father and the Mother made a Child. I am the elder of the Children, true – but now the younger rises to His Day.

38. The nature of true Alchemy is that it changes not alone the substance of the Work, but also changes thence the Alchemist. Ye whose Will it is to Work thereby, behold mine inverse image, and consider well its meaning for thy Task.

The Showing of the Image

39. From out of the Yonilingam drifted forth a Cloud, violet and light-shot. In the misty heart thereof a sound arose, vibrating soft, yet filling everywhere.

40. Jeweled and flashing rainbow-lights from wings, there hovered in the midst a humble BEE. Striped gold and brown, soft-haired and curved in form, it shone its eyes unto the Priests and Kings assembled.

41. Spoke then She-Who-Moves from out of the mist surrounding:

42. This is the symbol of the Work-to-come, the Great Gynander in its Earthly form. The Magickian shall grow like unto the BEE as the Æon unfolds, a leader and sign unto the Race of Man.

43. What then of its nature doth the BEE show forth?

44. Behold, it is not male nor female in the singular. It labors forth by day in constant flight, an egoless do-er, whose will and the Hive Will are but one.

45. It gathers up the flower-nectar, flies to Hive and there, in pure Comm-Union, doth in its very body Transubstantiate.

46. The Nectar is now Honey. Bee to bee, it is transferred, speaking all Hive Mysteries from and to each mouth. By

the same mouth that first ingathered, is the honey spent, the secret Alchemy within the Centers turning Silver–Gold.

47. The Hive now lives, immortal. With queen and workers, drones and builder-bees, soldiers, foster-mothers – all are one. In constant life-renewal, the Hive breathes as One Being – for so indeed it is. In the Will of the Hive is the Will of the Bee fulfilled. Each in its appointed place, the Bees work out their Will in ordered harmony.

48. The image fades. Now the poised Plume moves in dancing fashion, unfolding from the center shaft long wings, transforming to the shape of the dark Vulture.

49. But know, O Children of the Hawk, a Man is not a Bee. He may profit from the image thereof, to learn of Wisdom in the Working. Behold in Me another image for thy heart's instruction.

50. There rose before their eyes the Tower of Silence, wherein the Lovers of Fire lay their dead.

51. The Vulture form alighted soft therein, and ate the flesh from the corpses, to the bone. The wind howled, desolate, in this fearsome place, fluttering the cerements about the ivory bones.

52. Silently, the Winged One stared, gore smeared about her beak. Into the eyes of each Priest there assembled, her baleful gaze did search. In perfect peace they beheld

her searching, for each, as Warrior, had made of Death a brother. Deliberately then, she unfolded out her wings, and took to the wind, and soared up from that place.

The Giving of the Word

53. Eternity then reigned, Infinite the veil that hung about them.

54. Somewhere, sometime, the veil parted for a moment, and She-Who-Moves strode forth. More comely than mortal woman ever was, She glowed in radiance of pearl and amethyst. Fine pleated linen was Her gown, girded in gold and silver, and on Her head, a nemyss of starred blue. Her crown was but a single plume, free-standing, and in her hands the Ankh and Wand of healing.

55. Unto each Warrior-Priest she moved, embraced and kissed them. Then, seated in the midst, She spoke as comrade equally-ranked:

"All ye who practise well the High Art, hearken. There shall be nothing hidden from thy sight. All formulae and Words shalt thou discover, being initiated by those whose Work it is to aid the Law of Will.

"What was given by Aiwaz is yet unfolding. There is much to do for slaves but newly freed into their Kingship, as ye well know. And each who Works within the Kingdom proceeds space, according to his Will.

56. "Ye have worked well in all that has been given; upon the

57. Tree of Life are ye founded. In Tetragrammaton have ye proceeded; in all the Beast hath given ye have practised well. Ye have become Hadit, and NU, and Ra-Hoor-Khuit also. As Heru-Pa-Kraath did ye abide in silence. Ye know PAN as lover and as godform, and BABALON is bride and self to you.

58. "The forces of Shaitan have ye engendered, calling forth the nexus of the ninety-three wherein to work your Will. Separation for the joy of Union have ye known, and Alchemy is Science to your Art.

59. "For those who know, and will, and dare, and keep in silence, it goes now further.

60. "In death is Life – for now as ever has it been so. The Willed Death is eternal – keep it so. Self of Ego, selfson born of Maya, must be slain on the moment of birth. The unsleeping Eye must vigil keep, O Warriors, for the illusion is self-generate.

61. "Constant watchfulness is the first Act – the Abyss is crossed by minutes, every day.

62. "If ye would dance the Mask, then mask the Dance. Exquisite must be the Art in this wise; and balance in the Center be maintained, or else ye shall give unwonted Life unto thine own creations. Tread carefully this path of Working, Mage. A tool, by Will devised, makes an ill master.

63. "Now in the Mass, the Eagle must be fed upon what she has shared in making. By the same mouth that roars upon the

mountain, is the word-act of No Difference given.

64. "And when Will declares, therein shall join the BEE to add the gold to red and white. The essence of Shaitan is Nectar here, the Temple is the Hive. The Lion is the Flower, now betimes, the Eagle invokes the nature of the BEE.

65. "Within the triple-chambered shrine is the first nectar pooled. The summons of the wand of PAN awakens the portal – opening bliss. And from the third and inmost chamber, in joy supreme, the Sothis-gift, quintessential mead, bounds forth to join Eagle-tears and Lion-blood.

66. "Solve et Coagula. Comm-Union thereby, whereof the Cosmos itself dissolveth, and re-forms by Will. And know, if aught can be so ordered in the Kingdom, that three or more is zero, as well as older truths."

67. Then stirred the Warrior-Priests, and of their number, a nameless one stepped forth.

68. "We know thee, Lady, unspoken though Thy name has been thus far. But say now – what was written on the manskin? What is the word Thou givest?"

69. She smiled and drew from out her robe a parchment scroll, shaped even as a Star. Unrolling it, She turned it roundabout, so all might see.

70. IPSOS

71. "What is this Word, O Lady – how may it be used?"

72. "In silent wisdom, King and Warrior-Priest. Let the deed shine forth and let the word be hidden; the deed is lamp enough to veil the face.

73. "It is the word of the twenty-third path, whose number is fifty and six. It is the unspoken Abode, wherein the Dance of the Mask is taught by Me. Tahuti watches without the Ape; I am the Vulture also.

74. "It is the Chalice of Air and Wand of Water, the Sword of Earth and Pantacle of Fire. It is the hourglass and tail-biting serpent. It is the Ganges becoming Ocean, the Way of the Eternal Child.

75. "It names the Source of Mine Own Being – and yours. It is the origin of this sending, that channels through Andromeda and Set. What race of gods do speak to Man, O Willed Ones? The word of them is both the Name and the Fact.

76. "It is for thee mantram and incantation. To speak it is to bring about certain change. Be circumspect in its usage – for if its truth be known abroad, it would perchance drive the slaves to madness and despair.

77. "Only a true Priest-King may know it fully, and stay in balance through his GO-ing flight. This is all I speak for now. The Book of the Preshadowing of the Feather is complete. Do what thou wilt shall be the whole of the Law. Love is the law, love under will."

DONAT PER OMNE · SCRIBA: NEMA

SOL IN CAPRICORNUS · ANNO HERU LXX · CINCINNATI

Appendix B

I've written a number of commentaries on *Liber Pennae Praenumbra* over the years, attempting to explain the more obscure words and passages of its specialized language and spirit. As a received document, the information was forced into its manifested form by my own shortcomings, by my lack of experience, and by my immersion in the Victorian/King James Bible style of the writings of Aleister Crowley.

This time, I was inspired to translate it into a simpler and more universal English. This serves the purpose of a commentary, in my opinion. Proper names of entities and certain technical terms can be found in the Glossary. Even in the simpler language I've found myself writing in poetic meter and occasional rhyme, but this seems proper to the subject matter. I've chosen not to use a Latin title for this new look at an eternal subject; I call it *Feathersong*.

Feathersong

1. These words rise from eternity:

2. Lady of air, upon which sails the sun-god's boat, the same mouth speaks and drinks. Lady of spiritual balance, the same mouth creates and devours.

3. All means of our linking with the world through perception, nourishment, and love, can be symbolized in and by the mouth. Your cosmos is so beautiful!

4. All lovers lost in each other salute you, light beyond human sight, whose nature can change the inner self. As the sense of self diminishes, the flow of cosmic energy through one increases. Tell us, the children of the future, what you desire. Tell us of your love.

5. Speaks the balance of motion:

6. I fly to you, you who do your will. Blessed are you who love under will and who give all of yourself to the universe. As Isis gathered the pieces of Osiris' body, so you pursue your history. By understanding the past, you conceive the vision of what mankind should be. You work to bring this vision to actuality.

7. The future you seek to manifest will sustain and pleasure you, when men and women war no more. Working to transcend your present state brings joy; those working together to transcend will be more successful than many working individually.

8. The institutions of control belong to the past; the twentieth century has seen the rise of individual freedom and responsibility. The future belongs to the innocent and the open-minded, to those who live gladly in the flow of things.

9. The scribe, as self-appointed critic and representative for humanity, speaks:

10. What are these words? An Aeon is supposed to last two thousand years. The era of spiritual and political submission

just ended in this century with its birth of the spirit of individual sovereignty. This spirit has just begun its work.

11. The Lady is amused, but kind.

12. The spirit of the new age, like a hunting hawk, still flies in the sun, enlightening and encouraging those who watch and love him. But—how does this hawk fly? By the air (and I am Lady of the air) and by the feathers of his wings (and the feather is my special symbol).

13. Time is as stable as it ever was, and history within it, implacable as Saturn/Set, the Lord of time and necessity. The hero-hawk will fly for as long as his work remains the death of restriction and servility.

14. Again, the scribe:

15. Am I mistaken, then to think your Aeon is to follow his? Are you not Maat?

16. Again, the Lady is amused.

17. At times you see me as truth personified; at other times I can be seen as maiden, mother, and crone, or as the veils of nothing, limitlessness and limitless light. Do not confuse yourself in my varied appearances; truth rules.

18. I cannot be caged. Who can bar my way or stop my advent when time and space are my own servants?

19. In fact, scribe, you need me to speak. The same mouth that breathes my air gives voice to doubts. Know me in silence–I come to further enlighten the doers of will.

THE WORD OF FLIGHT

20. Your balance is maintained by forward motion; never tell yourself that you've arrived.

21. When you abandoned old ways of control, their institutions were already dying. In your questings for the truth you've found a resonance in symbols of the birds.

22. Crowned in silence on a starry sea,
    serenely glides the Swan, forever free.

    Balanced on one foot where sea meets shore,
    the Heron ponders wisdom evermore.

    The great eyes of the Owl can understand
    the ways of hunting in a night-dark land.

    The Raven's call for mercy must be heard
    in honor of the ebon battle-bird.

    With strength of trumpets in his greeting cry,
    the Cockerel hails light in eastern sky.

    Soaring in the sunrise, beauty-bright,
    the Hawk enraptures all who see his flight.

Appendix B :: Feathersong

In victory the Peacock spreads his fan,
a thousand eyes of love he shows to man.

Swift as thought and splendid as a flower,
the Hummingbird's a flying jewel of power.

The dreamers heed the haunting call of Loon,
founded in the dusk of mist and moon.

Beneath her wings the Eagle's kingdom flows,
as to her mystic lover Lion she goes.

Alchemic union changes her to Swan—
with realm and crown conjoined she travels on.

The Ibis on the verge of starless deeps
unveils the secret knowledge that he keeps.

23. From them you learned to fly, my noble souls, as you fly now within the sea of stars. Beware of danger, though, from traitors and from those who envy you, who would abort your flight.

24. Contemplate your heart and judge yourself. If you are honest, your heart weighs no more than does my feather-form. It will not pull you down the starless deeps. Alchemic gold is light, but inert lead of unjust deeds will bind you to the ground. Search deeply for your inner nature.

25. If anything would hinder you, it is your *doing*; let action do itself. See this teaching now within the Temple.

26. So saying, the balance of motion assumed the appearance of the great Black Flame, the light beyond sight, growing from the feather-shaft and billowing out into the Void. The doers of will watched silently, and listened to her words form in their hearts.

27. Look well! This lens of stars, this galaxy, is the one named Andromeda. Through it, I, the balance of motion, the Magickal Current, flow to the Sirius system, then to your Sun, then to your individual selves.

28. The work of transformation lasts a lifetime. In cosmic love and innate will do everything. Through compassion understand your primal self. From the center of your self embrace the universe.

29. Do this, then go farther. Lose all that is not you, that separates your essence from the ineffable. If anything or anyone would capture you, leave the part they grasp, like empty clothing, and *go*, a naked soul.

30. Now you gather in our sacred space, as guides of the spiritually hungry, as doers of will, as defenders of truth, as changers of manifestations. The flow of things, the Tao, the truth, is found in transformations.

31. The Ibis-headed Thoth, cosmic scribe and Lord of science, gives the basic keys of world and spirit. Chthonos underlies matter-energy; learn its essence, control its power. Ychronos is true eternity, in which lies time and the dimensions beyond it.

32. These two keys are one, the essence of the physical world. They are the keys of transmutation and of the power of the elements.

33. The assembly received the keys, taking them to heart. The Black Flame danced and dwindled, becoming a quill-pen. There being nothing on which to write, one of the assembly laid his body's skin upon the altar as a living parchment. (In visions are great wonders, as in dreams.)

34. The Lady wrote on it a word, but did not show it to them. In patience the gathering did wait, knowing that in time they'd have the word.

35. Again the quill-pen grew, taking on the form of the Yonilingam. From this sign of male and female unity arose the image of Baphomet, who spoke:

36. You know the secrets of sexual Alchemy. You've lived and loved as universe and self, as Nature's lord and Lady of willed love. You also know my nature, the androgyne, hermaphroditic archetype.

37. Two main genders has the human race; the man and woman generate the child. I am the older of the children, containing beast and human, male and female. My younger brother, human Horus, charismatic warrior, enlightens now the world.

38. True Alchemy, in changing substances through love, changes also the Alchemists. If you would work this way, learn from my sister-opposite.

THE SHOWING OF THE IMAGE

39. From the Yonilingam rose a cloud of sparkling violet, from which came a soft vibration.

40. Striped in amber and burnt umber,
    eyes of jewels, rainbow wings,
    as you hover, so we wonder,
    loving honey, fearing stings.

41. The Lady's voice rings from the violet cloud:

42. This is a symbol of your future's Work. Take note of how the Bee suggests a way of living suited to large human numbers.

43. In what ways does the Bee's nature teach us?

44. The worker bee is neither male nor female, even though it's female in its form. For all its life its joy is in the hive; it labors for the benefit of all.

45. Flower to flower does it fly, nectar drinker, pollen captor, then to hive. Within its body, it changes nectar's nature.

46. The nectar is now honey, circulating to and from each mouth. In the taste of message molecules, each bee knows the state and health of all. By the same mouth that gathered up the nectar, is the honey spent. In process and in circulation then, does food become an information chain.

47. The hive's alive, a being in itself, immortal as a bee sees it, and home. Queen and larva, nurse and guard, honey-bringer, builder of the comb, old one fanning wings in doorway wait the fatal bridal flight of drone. In the will of the hive is the will of the bee fulfilled. The task of each age is where the bee finds joy.

48. The image fades. The Black Flame-feather dances, growing wings, becoming the dark vulture.

49. But be aware, you who do your will, a man is not a bee. Humans can profit from Nature's examples, but never take a metaphor too far. Watch me for another image.

50. A vision rose—the Tower of Silence where the Parsis lay their dead. The fire and the earth, too sacred for a corpse, bade them offer such to air and bird.

51. The vulture lit upon the Tower and ate the flesh from corpses, to the bone. The wind howled, desolate, fluttering the corpse-cloth about the ivory bones.

52. Into the eyes of each of the assembly the blood-stained vulture stared. They each returned her gaze in peaceful silence. None of them feared death; each had embraced it. The vulture spread her wings, took to the wind, and soared up from the Tower.

The Giving of the Word

53. Eternal, infinite, a veil enclosed them.

54. Time began again as the veil parted;
    infinity became a woman's form.
    More beautiful she was than mortal woman;
    her light of amethyst and pearl shone warm.
    Her gown was made of fine Egyptian linen,
    about her waist were wings of silver-gold.
    Her headdress, midnight blue with stars of diamond,
    a circlet and her single plume did hold.
    In one hand was the Ankh, the *crux ansata*,
    the sandal-strap of gods who live to Go.
    The other held a wand of woven serpents,
    the healing-rod of Thoth from long ago.

55. She moved among the gathered seekers, embraced and kissed each one. She sat with them and spoke as though with equals.

56. Listen to me, mages; hear me, sages. Nothing will be hidden from your sight. All patterns of rites and words of power will be yours. Heed the counsel of your elders on the path.

57. You've done well in your learning. You understand the Tree of Life and its Qaballah; you comprehend the Tetragrammaton. You know willed love and how to use its power. You have become the secret Self, and Cosmos, and Horus, warrior of will. As Harpocrat, you kept yourself in

silence. You've loved Pan and you've been Pan; you've loved and been the Lady Babalon.

58. You've raised and used the darker powers of Set-Shaitan-Saturn-Shiva, to link with Horus in the work of will. You've seen yourself as separate from the cosmos so in your union with it you find joy. Experiments in mind and body point the way for creativity.

59. There's more to learn, my noble souls, even as you know, and will, and dare, and keep in silence.

60. In death is life, as Nature's cycles show us. Deliberated death of self's illusion takes you out of time; continue this. The self of ego, this illusion of identity, must die each time it forms. Be vigilant, since this illusion generates itself.

61. Keep a constant watch–the Abyss is crossed by minutes, every day.

62. If you would dance the Mask, then mask the Dance. Your art must excel in making selves to fit your audience, be it human, Other, or you, yourself. Your natural self's unreal, the Masks are even less. Maintain a dancing balance in their making, lest they convince you they contain your essence. A tool, devised by will, makes a bad master.

63. In Alchemy are partners equal, the lunar Eagle and the solar Lion. By the same mouth roaring on the mountain is this equity acknowledged.

64. When you choose, invoke the Bee to join its golden sacrament of hive to Lion's red of male and Eagle's white of female. Nectar is the seed, the temple-hive's the womb, the nectar is the Lion's and the Eagle acts as Bee.

65. Within her heart and self this gathered nectar fountains up and pools. Then Lion rises, summoning new bliss. And from the third and inmost temple-chamber flows the charged nectar, golden mead, to join the Eagle's tears and Lion's blood.

66. Dissolve in the selflessness of psychic death and then reform as will and work requires, in rebirth more than resurrection. This is the sacrament by which the Cosmos dissolves and reforms by will. And know, upon the plane of earth, that three or more is zero, as well as other truths.

67. The assembled ones then stirred, and from their ranks a nameless one stepped forward.

68. We know you, Lady, unspoken though your name has been thus far. But say now–what was written on the manskin? What is this word you give?

69. She smiled, and drew from her robe a parchment scroll shaped as a star (for every man and every woman is a star). Unrolling it, she turned it roundabout, so all might see.

70. IPSOS

71. What is the word, O Lady–how may it be used?

72. In silent wisdom, noble soul. Let the deed shine forth and let the word be hidden; the deed is lamp enough to veil the face.

73. It's the word of the twenty-third path that leads beyond the Tree. Its number is given as fifty-six, the day of dread beauty to come when everything changes. It is the unspoken abode, where I whisper its dance of the Mask. Tehuti keeps watch with his Ape, recording without opinion. I am the vulture also, sharing the prey of the hawk.

74. It is the Chalice of Air and Wand of Water, the Sword of Earth and Pantacle of fire. In it are contradictions reconciled. It is the hourglass and the tail-biting serpent, Ouroboros, mighty in time and in eternity. It is the Ganges becoming ocean, the Way of the Eternal Child, which is the Tao of Lao Tze.

75. It names my source–and yours. It is the origin of this sending, which flows through Andromeda and Sirius. What race of gods speak to mankind, my willed ones? The word of them is both the name and fact.

76. It is for you a mantram and incantation. To speak it is to bring certain change. Take care in using it. If its truth be widely known at this time, it could drive the sleepers to madness and despair.

77. Only the awakened can understand it fully and use it wisely. This is all I speak for now. The book of the preshadowing

of the feather is complete. Do what thou wilt shall be the whole of the law. Love is the law, love under will.

> GIVEN THROUGH ALL
>
> WRITTEN BY NEMA
>
> SUN IN CAPRICORN, 1974 C.E.
>
> CINCINNATI

Glossary

Adept
Adjective: skillful; noun: a person in the second stage of inner progress that I divide into Initiate, Adept, and Priest. The Initiate learns truths and processes about nonphysical reality, the Adept applies the knowledge to him/herself and to the world, and the Priest assists others to learn and practice.

Akashic Record
An account of personal, planetary, and universal history that exists beyond time in the realm of Akasha/Spirit. One can find it and read its contents in the upper astral planes in trance state, with appropriate instruction and practice.

Anthropic
Of or pertaining to humans.

Astral
Literally, "starry." Used as noun and as adjective, it refers to the place/plane/condition of dreams, emotions, and templates of physical beings. Although it seems shadowy to our normal way of seeing things, it's the base or foundation of the physical world.

Banishment
A process of clearing and cleaning an area, object, or structure of random, distracting, and/or antagonistic energies and entities.

Banishment after a rite or a meditation restores balance to the atmosphere of a place.

Belief
An idea held to be true without proof. Faith.

Ceremonial Magick
A process of obtaining knowledge and of causing change by means of detailed rituals and practices.

Chakra
Sometimes pronounced "kakra," a chakra is a center or node of energy flow in individuals and planets. In humans, the major chakras are in or near the anus/perineum, the genitals, the navel/solar plexus, the heart, the throat, the center of the forehead and the crown of the head. I add the point at the back of the head to make a total of eight.

Contemplation
The process of regarding an idea or object without analysis or judgment; silent observation.

Cosmophilia
Love of all existence.

Deep Mind
A term I first heard from Jan Fries that I consider to mean the intelligence of all existence. Individuals can become aware of their participation in it and use it to think and intuit far beyond their individual capacities.

Deva
Originally, a divine being. I use it in the specialized sense of the spirit or persona of the collective consciousness of a species, be it mineral, vegetable, animal, or other. It guards its species through peril and want, and it can be consulted to find the true needs of its species. For example, a gardener would be wise to commune with the corn deva, the pea deva, the thyme deva, and so on, to find out how best to raise his or her vegetables, herbs, and flowers. All that's needed to do this is to call politely to the deva to help you, then listen carefully.

Double Consciousness
The simultaneous presence in the mind of one's familiar individuality and of our genus' unity. The common consciousness acts as a vehicle for world-wide empathy, selective telepathy, and awareness of our own genus. A state of triple consciousness is obtained when one's personal sense of unity extends beyond humanity to include all life. Whatever is, lives; whatever lives is intelligent.

Ecstasy
A condition of suspended senses, thinking, and motion rising from overwhelming emotional response (most often pleasurable) to revelations larger than one's usual view of oneself and of the cosmos.

Elements
In esoteric Western tradition, the elements are fire, water, air, earth, and spirit. In some Eastern traditions, wood and metal are included as elements. Unlike the elements of the periodic table of chemistry, which describe a level of the physical plane,

the esoteric elements describe the character of an idea, entity, person, place, or thing. Most of these can be described by two or more elements in combination.

Etheric
Pertaining to the ether that, according to ancient Western tradition, fills the space between the stars and permeates the physical plane. Invisible and intangible, the ether was supposed to be the medium by which certain forces worked on physical objects. I consider the ether a medium in which the ideas or concepts of things are found. In my experience, it's less dense, or farther from the physical world, than are the astral planes.

Forgotten Ones
The major survival instincts of humans that are stronger and more influential on our thoughts and actions than we credit them. They are hunger, sex, fight-or-flight, clanning, communication, curiosity, altruism, and desire for transcendence. (See Chapter 2.)

Fractal
A noun and an adjective devised by Benoit Mandelbrot to indicate his new geometry based on Chaos Science. This geometry describes recurrent elaborations of patterns in formations that resemble fern leaves, paisley, snow flakes, coastlines, and so on.

Gematria
The process of determining the hidden meanings and associations of words by their numerical value in alphabets that use letters to represent numbers, such as Hebrew, Arabic, and Greek. The

total of the letters' number values equals the value of the entire word. Words that share a number value are related in subtle or obvious ways; if a received word's number corresponds with the number values of ideas that are harmonious with a similar meaning of the received word, you can trust that it's genuine or valid, pending proof to the contrary. For more details, see the "Practicum: Banishment" section in Chapter 11.

Horoscope

An astrological chart outlining the positions of the planets within the signs of the zodiac and in relationship with each other for a given earthly location, day, and time. Currently, horoscopes are most often cast for individuals' place and time of birth, although the correct timing and location for important events also can be determined astrologically. The operation of a horoscope presupposes that planetary positions influence events or conditions the subject will encounter in a given span of time.

IChing/Yking

A Chinese system of divination using the tossing and the patterns of the fall of yarrow stalks or of three coins to designate lines of four types: Old Yin, Old Yang, Young Yin, and Young Yang. Yin lines have a break in the middle (_ _), while Yang lines are solid (____). Old lines change into their opposites for a second formation, while young lines remain the same.

The lines are scribed from the bottom up in a stack to form any of eight trigrams; the trigrams combine to form any of sixty-four hexagrams. Each hexagram has an oracle assigned to it and to the meaning of any changing lines it contains. When the lines change, a new hexagram is formed. This new hexagram

often concerns itself with advice or with the consequences of the first hexagram. There are a number of books available about the I Ching, but my favorite remains *The I Ching or Book of Changes*, translated from Chinese to German by Richard Wilhelm, and translated from German to English by Cary F. Bayes, with a foreword by Carl Jung.

INITIATE, INITIATION

An Initiate is a person who has begun the search for inner truth and who is in the process of learning techniques and principles through study and practice. Initiation is the process in which one discovers a new view of everything, a larger context for understanding and wisdom.

INTUITION

That process by which our intelligence reaches a correct conclusion using less data than that required by reason. Hunch.

INSTINCT

A set of behaviors seemingly inborn, or genetically based, that act to preserve life, health, and species continuity. Instinct operates without needing prior thought or reasoning, although humans often rationalize their instinctive actions afterward.

JULIA SETS

A class of shapes invented and studied by Gaston Julia and Pierre Fatou; the familiar Mandelbrot set of Chaos Science contains Julia sets. The Julia sets are shaped like snowflakes, paisley designs, lightning bolts, and pinwheel galaxies.

KOAN

A paradoxical question or proposition designed to trap

reason long enough for intuition to grasp its meaning. It's a Buddhist technique for bypassing rational mind and attaining enlightenment.

Loa
A singular and plural term for the spirits of gods of Voodoo who are accessible to devotees through offerings and ritual possession.

Magick
According to Aleister Crowley, Magick is "the Science and the Art of causing change to occur in conformity with Will." Magick is a philosophy and behavior system that aids personal transcendence in the Magickian under the guise of his or her changing situations or events "external" to him or her.

Mandelbrot Set
A geometric pattern of internal repetitions that varies slightly in each recurrence. The not-quite-identical shapes appear in the border areas of the main figure, which resembles a spiky spider in foam.

Manicheanism
The belief that spirit is good and matter is evil. A sect teaching that spirit could win release from matter through asceticism was founded by Manes of Persia in 276 C.E.

Mantra
A word that is repeatedly spoken, chanted, or thought in order to engage the rational mind. When the mind is engaged in

following the mantra, intuitive or visionary information is more easily perceived.

Meditation

A practice of turning one's attention inward, quieting sensory information and rational thought through breath control and/or repetition of a mantra. Realizations/insights appear in the unoccupied awareness.

Metaphor

A word or concept used as a substitution for or description of another word or concept. It serves to illumine the original idea through its suggestion of a likeness between them.

Neter

An Egyptian concept of a god as a representation of a quality or principle depicted in human, animal, or in combination form. A few are imaged in other ways, such as the solar disk of Aten or the *utchet*, or eye.

Neti-Neti

"Not this-not this." A meditation for finding the essence of the self by discarding as not-self all things that can be considered possessions of the self.

Pranayama

The practice of regulating one's breathing in ways that affect the consciousness through physiological changes. The usual approach is to slow the breath by counting the inhalations and exhalations, often placing pauses of equal length between them. It's also possible to mentally repeat a mantra for the timing:

slowing the breathing calms the mind. In contrast, the Breath of Fire is a rapid series of inhalations and exhalations that serve to energize and charge body and consciousness.

PSI PHENOMENA
Blanket term for abilities that operate outside the realm of physical sensoria and action, such as telepathy (mind-to-mind communication), telekinesis (moving objects without physically touching them or using tools to do so), precognition (knowing events before they occur), clairvoyance (seeing events at a distance without instruments), and so on.

PHILOSOPHY
A system of thought based upon certain principles derived from a mix of observed events and opinions about them.

QABALLAH
An ordering of experience developed by Jewish mystics beginning in the sixth century B.C.E. and continuing to the present. Two salient features of Qaballah are the Tree of Life and the art of Gematria, the first being a map of spirit and the second a means of discovering relationships between or among words according to their numerical values.

RACIAL UNCONSCIOUS
A concept presented by psychologist Carl Jung stating that in addition to individual consciousness and an individual unconscious, humans share a species, or racial state of cognition he termed the Racial Unconsciousness. In it are found archetypes of myths and pantheons, characters whose qualities are found in all ethnic traditions.

Rapture
The state of being lifted out of oneself, of being taken from ordinary consciousness into a condition of thought-suspended wonder.

Reflection
The quiet beholding of a thought, image, or entity, to the end of increasing one's understanding of it. Reflection generates ideas about its object, which are then integrated into new knowledge. It's a more active process than contemplation.

Reincarnation
The process whereby one's identity finds a new physical body after death. Usually associated with the idea of karma (deeds), reincarnation provides a means of balance, justice, and education from life to life through various kinds of social and physical conditions into which one can be born.

Ritual
A series of actions performed to effect internal or external change, to celebrate seasonal feast days, or to mark life passages. Rituals can be done alone, with another person, or with a group; they can be held indoors or outdoors, can be silent, or can include words, chanting, drumming, or music. They can be formally scripted or spontaneous, can be performed once or in an extended program of repetition, and can include special instruments, robes, incense, and candles, or can be done nude and barehanded.

Servitor
An artificial entity created to perform automatic, constant, or

repetitive tasks on nonphysical levels.

Shaman
A person who undertakes spirit journeys to obtain knowledge, wisdom, and power from nonphysical levels of reality, then returns to the waking world to apply them to his or her community in terms of healing and prophecy.

Singularity
A point at which space and time are infinitely distorted by gravitational forces and which is held to be the final state of matter falling into a black hole. It's also used to designate the point of origin of the Big Bang, which produced the universe.

Stigmata
Physical marks appearing on a person's body with no physical cause. Certain Christian mystics, for example, exhibited marks on their hands and feet that imitated the nail-holes of the crucified Christ.

Strange Attractor
A term in Chaos Science that means a pattern of orbits in phase space that describes all possible behaviors of a dynamic system. This pattern is stable, low-dimensional, and nonperiodic. It is the trajectory toward which all other trajectories converge.

Tarot
A deck of seventy-eight cards used for divination, which has four suits: Wands/Rods, Cups, Swords, and Disks/Pentacles. The "small" cards in each suit are numbered from one to ten; a suit also has four royal cards: Kings, Queens, Princes, and

Princesses/Pages. There are twenty-two trump cards, or atus, which correspond to the twenty-two letters in the Hebrew alphabet. The cards are shuffled and laid out in patterns where meaning is derived from a card's position in the pattern.

Temple
A building or room dedicated to spiritual or religious activities.

Tetragrammaton
The "word of four letters," IHVH, that is a name or designation of God. The I, or Yod, represents the Father; the first H, or He', is the Mother; the V, or Vav, symbolizes the Son, and the final He' is the Daughter. In Hebrew tradition, IHVH is never spoken aloud; the word "Adonai" is used in its place.

THAT
The essence of being about which nothing true can be spoken. A traditional saying: "Thou art THAT, I am THAT, all this is THAT."

Thelema
A Greek word meaning "will." Aleister Crowley named his system of Magick Thelema, and stated its basic principles as "Do what thou wilt shall be the whole of the Law; love is the law, love under will." One's true will is the guiding theme of life and decisions; individuals must discover what their true will is and then devote themselves to doing it.

Trance
A suspension of ordinary consciousness in which attention is directed away from the physical world and toward inner visions

and information. It can be induced by repetition of a word, of rhythmical bodily movement, and of patterns of drumbeats and music. A person in trance becomes aware of levels of being often masked by the immediacy of daily living.

Transcendence
A rising beyond one's normal state of awareness into one that is more comprehensive, inclusive, and expansive.

Universal Pattern of Consciousness
A system of information gathering and processing that resembles a web or net of nodes in multiple contact with each other. It seems to follow the tendency of simplicity developing complexities through experience.

Water Dowsing
The process of detecting underground streams, springs, and aquifers, usually employing a forked stick or a pair of free-swinging rods that react by dipping downward or by forming a straight line when the person holding them walks over the site. The same process can be used to find buried conduits, electric lines, and various mineral deposits.

Will
The faculty of direction and decision-making based on an individual's inherent nature, talent, and desire. Finding and following one's true will creates the emotional condition called happiness.

WORD OF POWER

A word vibrated at full voice, whispered, spoken forcefully, or chanted at the climax of a magickal rite to seal and send an intention of change out into the world. It is charged with potency by being the name of a supernatural entity, or is a formula of process aligned with the nature of the rite.

Bibliography

Anonymous. *New American Standard Bible*. La Habra, Calif.: Foundation Publications Inc., 1998.

—. *The Holy Scriptures* (According to the Masoretic Text). Philadelphia: The Jewish Publication Society of America, 1955.

—. *The I Ching or Book of Changes*. Translated by Richard Wilhelm and Cary F. Baynes with a foreword by C.G. Jung. Princeton, N.J.: Princeton University Press, 1981.

Crowley, Aleister. *777 and Other Qabalistic Writings of Aleister Crowley*. New York: Samuel Weiser, Inc., 1979.

Fort, Charles. *The Complete Books of Charles Fort*. New York: Dover Publications, 1975.

Fries, Jan. *Visual Magick: A Manual of Freestyle Shamanism*. Oxford, England: Mandrake, 1992.

—. *Helrunar: A Manual of Rune Magick*. Oxford, England: Mandrake, 1993.

—. *Seidways: Shaking, Swaying and Serpent Mysteries*. Oxford, England: Mandrake, 1996.

—. *Living Midnight: Three Movements of the Tao*. Oxford, England: Mandrake, 1998.

Gleick, James. *Chaos: Making a New Science.* New York: Viking Penguin Inc., 1987.

Grant, Kenneth. *Outer Gateways.* London: Skoob Books Publishing, 1992.

—. *Outside the Circles of Time.* London: Frederick Muller Ltd., 1980.

—. *Zos Speaks! Encounters with Austin Osman Spare.* London: Fulgur Limited, 1998.

Hawking, Stephen. *Black Holes and Baby Universes and Other Essays.* New York: Bantam Books, 1993.

Horus Maat Lodge website: horusmaat.com: Virtual Magickal temple with rites at New Moon.

John of the Cross. *The Collected Works of St. John of the Cross.* Translated by Kieran Kavanaugh and Otilio Rodriguez. Washington D.C.: Nelson, 1991.

Kraig, Donald Michael. *Modern Magick: Eleven Lessons in the High Magickal Arts.* St. Paul, Minn.: Llewellyn Publications, 1989.

Kress, Kenneth A. *Parapsychology in Intelligence: A Personal Review and Conclusions;* Studies in Intelligence, CIA, 1977. Website: parascope.com/ds/articles/parapsychologyDoc.htm

Bibliography

Nema. *Maat Magick: A Guide to Self-Initiation.* York Beach, Maine: Samuel Weiser, Inc., 1995.

SilverStar: An electronic magazine with and for the curious. horusmaat.com/silverstar

Talbot, Michael. *The Holographic Universe.* New York: Harper Collins Publishers, 1991.

Teilhard de Chardin, Pierre. *The Phenomenon of Man.* Translated by Bernard Wall. New York: Harper, 1959.

Toffler, Alvin. *Future Shock.* New York: Random House, 1970.

INDEX

A

Abramelin Operation...163

Absolute Truth...133

Abyss...11, 195-201, 231-232, 261-262, 267, 278-279

Adept...175, 197, 202

Adversary...167, 170

aeon...229, 232, 263, 270-271

Akasha...257, 259, 283

Akashic Record...46, 124

alchemy...231, 261-262, 264, 266, 275, 279

Aleister Crowley...5-6, 51, 107, 114, 171, 197, 269, 289, 294, 297

ancestors...76, 95, 154, 160, 162, 170, 220

anthropic...17-18, 213, 283

Asatru...13

ascended masters...95

astral...25, 42, 65, 68, 80, 86, 95-97, 116-117, 120-126, 129, 131, 135, 137, 149-151, 161-163, 172-173, 175-178, 183, 189, 191, 196, 198, 202, 218-219, 283, 286

B

banish...74, 121, 126, 191

belief...19, 39, 46, 50, 104, 108-109, 112, 132, 160, 170, 220, 284, 289

Black Brother...197-198

Black Flame...257, 260, 262, 274-275, 277

Breath of Fire...290

C

censor...104, 131

ceremonial magick...6, 51, 68, 207, 284

chakra...35-38, 50, 84, 284

chaos mages...108

Chaos Science...286, 288, 293

Chaos Theory...156

circle...68, 75, 77, 80, 164, 203

Index

Contemplation . . .35, 63, 103, 108, 111, 119, 126, 284, 292

Cosmic Copier . . .160

Cosmophilia . . .39, 284

cosmos . . .10, 14, 20, 33-34, 41-42, 44, 136, 138, 143, 182-184, 208, 217, 267, 269, 278-280, 285

creation . . .30, 33, 43, 57, 121, 124, 129, 139, 141-142, 159, 170, 183, 228-229

Crowley, Aleister . . .297

Crusades . . .203

D

Dark Night of the Soul . . .11, 193-200

Deep Mind . . .16, 20, 24, 33, 46-47, 66, 69-70, 72-73, 97-98, 126, 135, 137, 190, 193, 220, 284

dervish . . .154

Deva . . .285

devil . . .30, 42-43, 170, 218, 230-231, 246

Double Consciousness . . .54, 215-217, 225, 285

E

earth . . .26, 28, 29, 37, 71, 75, 77-79, 87, 103, 123, 125, 141, 167, 189, 196, 205, 221, 228, 231, 261, 268, 277, 280, 281, 285

ecstacy . . .114

ego . . .91, 112, 188, 266, 279

Elementals . . .89, 218

Elements . . .18, 80, 125, 139, 161, 176, 214, 262, 275, 285, 286

ether . . .286

Etheric . . .42, 125, 161, 183, 286

F

faerie . . .42, 56, 231

fantasy life . . .143

fight-or-flight . . .7, 26, 38, 172-175, 286

Forgotten Ones . . .7, 20, 23, 25-26, 33, 35, 38, 172-174, 191, 286

fortune tellers . . .24

Fractal . . .42, 135, 286

Fries, Jan . . .297

G

Gematria . . .107, 113-114, 116-117, 286, 291

genus Homo . . .21, 205

god-forms . . .77, 81

God-hunger ...7, 23, 25, 31, 33-34, 38

gothic ...121

Grant, Kenneth ...298

Great Work ...195, 203, 205

Gypsy ...221

H

heaven ...28, 148, 160

hell ...130, 160, 194

Hermetic ...41, 138, 151

Higher Power ...95, 146

Holy Book ...11, 39

Holy Guardian Angel ...156, 163

horoscope ...84, 287

I

I Ching ...23, 84, 288, 297

initiate ...197, 228, 230, 232, 283, 288

inner ...9, 20, 21, 34, 36, 64-65, 70, 72-73, 86, 89, 97, 101, 103, 110, 146-148, 175, 187, 201-202, 204-205, 210, 225, 227, 260, 270, 273, 283, 288, 295

inner life ...103, 187, 201, 210

Instinct ...27, 30, 34-36, 38, 130, 132, 134, 147, 172-175, 198, 222, 288

intelligence ...14, 17, 24, 31, 34, 38, 43-44, 47, 53, 56-57, 70, 72, 86, 109, 121, 139, 140, 143-145, 147, 171, 174, 181, 185, 194, 197, 203-205, 216, 219, 220, 228, 284, 288, 298

K

Koan ...288

Kundalini ...35-37

L

Lady ...79, 261, 267, 269, 271, 275-276, 279-280

law ...18, 102, 178, 222-223, 258, 265, 268, 282, 294

life force ...197-198

life form ...215

Loa ...23, 289

Lord ...28-29, 77-79, 230, 258, 271, 274-275

Lovecraftian ...7, 121

lunar ...117, 150, 279

M

Maat Magick ...6, 49, 51-53, 56-58, 61, 76, 121, 230, 257, 298

mage . . .11, 98, 109, 111, 130, 136, 198, 205, 208, 266

magick . . .5-9, 13, 23, 30, 32, 45, 49-53, 56-57, 62, 68, 76, 89, 95, 101, 117, 119, 121, 127, 143, 198, 201-202, 204, 206-208, 218, 222-223, 226-227, 230, 232, 257, 284, 289, 294, 297-298

magickal . . .6-7, 9-10, 13, 41, 51, 53, 70, 104-105, 111, 120, 127, 157, 163, 178, 205-206, 208, 213, 227, 231, 274, 296, 298,

magickian . . .59, 95, 111, 136, 263, 289

Mandelbrot Set . . .41, 288-289

Manichean . . .43

mantra . . .36, 63, 69, 92, 119, 289-290

Master . . .46, 116, 120, 261

Maya . . .183, 229, 266

Meditation . . .27, 36, 63-64, 67, 69, 73, 92, 103, 108, 111, 119, 126, 187, 193, 215, 284, 290

messianic . . .110

metaphor . . .27, 39, 133, 148, 157, 163, 167-168, 181, 277, 290

metaphysical . . .19, 42, 96

miracle . . .102, 105

mystery . . .8-11, 13-15, 17-19, 25, 30-31, 33, 39-42, 44-46, 49-53, 54, 57, 59-60, 63-64, 66-73, 81, 83-84, 86-89, 92, 95-97, 101, 104, 108-111, 117, 119, 122, 126-127, 129-138, 140-141, 143-146, 148-153, 157, 159, 161, 167, 170-171, 174, 178-179, 181-182, 184-186, 188-196, 198-199, 201-202, 204-210, 213, 217, 220, 222-223, 231, 262

mystery-hunters . . .157, 204

mystical . . .11, 71, 81, 105, 157, 163, 198, 205, 208, 213

mystics . . .40, 57, 69, 133, 149-150, 156, 182, 188, 193, 203-204, 291, 293

N

N'Aton . . .215-217, 221, 225

nature . . .7, 9, 17-20, 26-27, 29, 42-43, 46, 50, 54-55, 64, 67, 70, 73, 92, 103, 110, 119, 123-125, 127, 130, 134-135, 137-138, 142, 144, 148-151, 157, 160, 163, 170-171, 174-175, 178, 185, 188-189, 192, 195, 197-198, 200, 209, 218, 220, 223, 226, 228, 230, 258, 260-263, 267, 270, 273, 275-277, 279, 295-296

neter . . .77, 290

neti-neti...145, 157, 182, 290

non-actions...96

Nothing...15, 97, 229

O

Old Ones...137

One True Way...133

ordeal...194, 199, 231

Order...59, 206, 226

outer...18, 63-64, 84, 102, 141-142, 188, 202, 225, 227

P

Parent...88

philosophy...8, 18-19, 30, 43, 144, 148, 167, 210, 226, 289, 291

poetry...27, 46, 121, 133-134, 154, 157, 181

pranayama...61, 63, 66, 69, 74, 290

precognition...24, 291

priest...264-265, 268, 283

probability-worlds...125, 143

Q

Qabalistic...51, 107, 297

Qlipoth...121

R

Racial Unconscious...54-55, 225, 291

rapture...37, 72, 110-111, 113, 136, 146-147, 149-152, 156, 164-165, 167, 175, 181, 185, 188-189, 190, 192-193, 196, 200, 207, 209, 292

reflection...23, 63, 292

reincarnation...160, 217, 292

ritual...36, 65, 68-69, 75, 79-80, 108, 121, 131, 163, 189, 227, 289, 292

S

Saturn...116-117, 271, 279

science...6, 17-19, 24, 30, 39, 41, 45, 55, 91, 95, 102, 134, 151, 171, 184, 195, 220-221, 226, 231, 266, 274, 286, 288-289, 293

servitor...292

Set...77, 259, 268, 271, 279

shaman...293

shamanism...297

shape-shifters...56

singularity...32, 139, 144, 182-183, 293

spacetime...21, 67, 149, 183-185

spheres...49, 101

sphinx...112

stigmata...147, 293

strange attractor...156, 293

subselves...155, 157, 159-164, 167, 175-176, 178

T

tao...204, 207, 274, 281, 297

tarot...10, 23, 51, 112, 225-226, 230, 293

telekinesis...24, 291

telepathy...24, 285, 291

temple...36-37, 51, 54, 67-74, 76, 81, 98-99, 116-117, 120, 123-124, 143, 207, 227, 259-261, 267, 273, 280, 294, 298

Teresa of Ávila...40

Tetragrammaton...51, 103, 265, 278, 294

That...41, 181-185, 187-188, 194, 204, 222

the Fates...117

the Observer...158-161

the Other...33

Thelema...51, 222, 294

Thelemic...51, 208

Thelemic Magick...51, 208

Theory of Everything...129

trance...111, 126, 140, 146, 150, 161, 165, 207, 214-215, 283, 294-295

transcendence...14, 25, 29, 38, 204, 210, 216, 286, 289, 295

transformation...13, 31, 53, 102, 109, 124, 165, 195, 205, 207, 222, 226, 230, 274

Tree of Life...49, 51, 84, 195, 221, 225, 265, 278, 291

Trickster...31, 202, 223

U

Universal Pattern of Consciousness...138, 295

universe...6-9, 15, 18-19, 25, 32-33, 35, 42-44, 47, 49, 56, 72, 89, 97-99, 103-104, 110, 134, 139-141, 143-144, 149, 151-153, 156, 158-159, 170, 174, 195-197, 202, 205-206, 213, 220, 226-227, 229, 232, 270, 274-275, 293, 299

V

Voodoo...289

W

water dowsing . . . 295

Western Land . . . 160

Wicca . . . 5, 13, 75, 207

witchcraft . . . 5

word of power . . . 62, 92, 296

world-view . . . 87, 132, 197, 206, 220

Z

zodiac . . . 225, 287

About the Book

Wings of Rapture takes a nondenominational approach to mysticism. From the initial euphoric experience to the "dark night of the soul" and beyond, this book will serve as a guide as you seek your own path to enlightenment.

Methods of altering consciousness to open the doors of perception to the metaphysical realms as well as techniques for creating sacred space conducive to successful meditation and contemplation are presented in a clear and lucid style.

If you're currently involved with an established religion, magickal order, coven, or popular spiritual teacher, it can help you slice through the embellishments of other people's visions to find your own.

This is a revised and expanded re-print of the book originally entitled *"The Way of Mystery: Magick, Mysticism and Self-Transcendence."*

About the Author

Nema encountered the works of Aleister Crowley in the early 1970s and became a member of Kenneth Grant's Typhonian Order for several years. During the same time period, she practiced group rituals with other magickians in Cincinnati, Ohio, and became a member of Bate Cabal, publisher of the *Cincinnati Journal of Ceremonial Magick*.

Nema was an experienced magickian and mystic, and the author of *Maat Magick* and *The Way of Mystery* (republished here as *Wings of Rapture*). She was an Elder and High Priestess of the Circle of the Sacred Grove, Church of Pantheist Wicca, and an initiate of Adi Nath Tantra. She was a founding member of the Horus-Maat Lodge – horusmaatlodge.com. Nema passed through the veil January, 9 2018.

www.ingramcontent.com/pod-product-compliance
Lightning Source LLC
Chambersburg PA
CBHW030851170426
43193CB00009BA/569